MAY I CALL YOU

QUEEN

UNLOCKING THE ROYALTY CODE
TO LIVING YOUR BEST LIFE

KEREL R. PINDER

MAY I CALL YOU
QUEEN

ISBN:978-0-9989921-2-9

Design by Mr. Michael J Maltuka of Basik Studios
Omaha, Nebraska USA

Printed in the USA.

Dear Kenny, this one is for you! I carry your laughter with me everyday! I am forever missing you.

ACKNOWLEDGMENTS

First, I would like to thank God for His amazing hand in my life. I truly appreciate the gift He has given me through writing. This year has been one of the hardest years of my life, there were honestly so many times when I thought writing this book wouldn't even be possible, but through God all things are possible.

To my parents, Peter and Joyce Pinder, thank you for being my pillar of support and a great source of wisdom. Thank you for supporting my dreams and for giving me the space to continue to soar unconventionally.

To my sister, Katheldra and brother-in-law: Lorrie, thank you for always opening your home and workspace for me to regain the peace and serenity that I need to allow my words to flow.

To my Guardian Angel Kenton thank you for teaching me gratitude, patience and a newfound meaning of love. I miss you dearly; your life has impacted mine in so many ways, I will love you forever brother.

To my first round of editors, Katheldra, Lynne, Ashleigh B, and Gail, thank you for devoting your time to this project. Your wisdom and insight truly influenced the pages of this book. I genuinely appreciate you; the clarity of this book would not be possible without you.

To the unnamed women whose stories are woven through the pages of this book, thank you for sharing your struggles and triumphs with me, but most of all thank you for teaching me the fabrics of a Queen.

To the team at Basik Studios, especially Michael & Sharrana Matulka, thank you for once again believing in my vision and helping me to package my purpose to present to the world.

Last but not least thank you, to you. To all of the wonderful women reading these pages, I want you to know that in every sense of the word, you are a Queen! Thank you for believing in my vision enough to not only purchase this book but to also read the words that I hope will leave you feeling inspired, motivated, and restored. So without further a due, let's begin

TABLE OF CONTENTS

PREFACE

I sat at my computer working on a script when an email popped up with this gorgeous couple on a YouTube video. It was the video invite to my friend's upcoming wedding. I pressed play instantly. You see, I'm a sucker for wedding websites, videos, photos, and all things love, so I had to check it out immediately. While I was excited for my friends and their upcoming nuptials, what stood out to me the most was the song playing in the background. It was Neyo's voice, but I had never heard the song before. I sat there and enjoyed the words: *"May I call you Queen, may I call you Queen."* This song captivated every part of me, but in 2.5 seconds I went from being happy for the couple to moping to Jesus about why I didn't have anybody to call me Queen. I pleaded, "I want somebody to call me Queen!"

Jesus said, "I call you Queen!" I felt a quick calming in my spirit. And He was right, He does. So why didn't I innately know this? Why did I feel having someone to call me Queen would automatically equate to happiness? And why would these thoughts come up again, even though at that moment I was assured by His love? Have you ever felt this way?

If so, why do you think we continuously pursue external things, expecting them to fill our every need, when in the end they don't? Why do we feel once we get married, have a baby, obtain our dream career, money, power or fame that everything in life will finally make sense? When in reality it won't.

1

I remember my third nomination for the Bahamian Icon Awards (slip in any famous award show you know; the Oscars, Emmys, The Tony's this the Bahamian equivalent of all of these shows wrapped into one.) I sat there in my 90 dollar Calvin Klein dress, waiting for the winner's name to be called. My college roommate, Kara who accompanied me to the event, told me to take my purse off my lap so that I could be ready to go up to the stage. I looked at her and said, "I lost this category twice already. I don't want to get my hopes up, let's wait." I closed my eyes, and seconds later, they were calling my name. I couldn't believe it, after losing twice in a row, I became so jaded about this process, I couldn't believe my ears.

I rushed to the stage and riddled off the speech I wrote while driving around in the car earlier that day. The crowd responded just as I expected them to, and I was grinning from ear to ear. The organizers quickly whisked me away to the place they take all the winners for photos and interviews. I was so happy! We went out for dinner and celebrated my achievement with friends. I was on cloud nine. However, about an hour into the dinner, that was it. The rush, the high, and excitement had already begun to fade away. Don't get me wrong, to this day I'm still incredibly grateful for the honor, and I'm proud of the work our team has been able to do, but that feeling of complete fulfillment was gone. I had been yearning for this moment since the first year I was nominated and it lasted for just a few hours. So, where did it go? Or better yet, why didn't it last?

Well, that's what I want us to talk about in this book. We will come face to face with the things that we think will make us happy; "the checklist", while exploring why they won't bring us the ultimate fulfillment we have been searching for and what actually will. So exactly how do we do this? Let's dive in and talk about it.

THE CHECKLIST

CHAPTER 1

MARRIAGE IS NO LONGER THE ULTIMATE GOAL

Daughters of Jerusalem, I charge you: Do
not arouse or awaken love until it so desires.

- Songs of Solomon 8:4 NIV

In 2016 God allowed me to release my first book, *The One Year Challenge: A New Journey to Love, Purpose, and Courtship!* I didn't want to write the book when God first told me to because I wanted it to end with a happy ending of me getting married with kids, and that hadn't happened yet. The crazy thing is my potential readers wanted the same thing. You know how hard it is to sell a book without a clear 'happy ending'? I would be selling my books at a booth. I would give my book pitch, it went like this, And Scene: "I took a year off of dating to focus on God and learning how to love myself. The One Year Challenge talks about my journey and the many lessons God taught me along the way." End Scene! And when I was done, I would have people look at me with hopeful eyes and say, "And then what? Are you married now? You found the guy?" And then I would politely smile and say, "No, but I found me!" And even though I sold hundreds of copies and received tons of great reviews, I still didn't feel complete. Some readers weren't buying it; they would give a nervous grin and say, "Oh ok," and then walk away, like no thanks! No one year challenge for me! I'm like, "see Jesus, I told you!"

I had grown during that year more than I ever did before, but sometimes that year made me upset. I had taken the year off, and I'd learned the lessons. By that time I had been celibate at the time for over three years, so why wasn't God blessing me?

That's how it works right? You stop having sex, you go to church every Sunday and serve in a few ministries and boom! God blesses your faithfulness. Nope! I was staring at 30, broken, confused, and single. Years later, God would show me that not getting married in my 20's was one of the best things that could ever happen to me. If you are reading this and you are in your 20's, you are probably secretly praying this is not the same fate God has designed for you and that's okay, I get it! I was that girl. So don't get me wrong, I'm not saying not getting married in your 20's will be the best thing that could ever happen to you. I just want to shed light on why it wasn't the best move for me and how we sometimes allow relationships to validate our worth.

For most of my life, getting married was one of the only goals I truly cared about and when I became serious about my faith, I still 'idolized' marriage. I just idolized it in a 'godly' way. You know the drill, "I want to get married so we can be on fire for God, fulfill our purpose together and make cute Youtube videos where we also inspire others to believe in Christ. God this isn't about me at all, I want to be married for you. So yeah, hurry up." The only person that bought that lie was me. God knew I would still revolve my life around an imperfect man and that I'd only seek him when my desires were not met. So if a marriage wouldn't complete me, why did I think it would? What thought patterns did I develop over the years that made me think that marriage would lead to a lifelong fulfillment? Here are the reasons God revealed to me why we often fall prey to seeking validation through relationships.

Generational Roots

In my first book, the *"The One Year Challenge"*, I talked a lot about how I was the little girl who dreamed of wedding dresses and happily-ever-afters. So I asked God what was it? I had the biggest crush on this boy from preschool up until the third grade crush on this boy in preschool up until the third grade. At this time, the biggest issue for me should have been what letter came after P in the alphabet and what toy I was going to play with at recess, but I was busy being devastated by the fact that this freckled face little boy had a girlfriend that wasn't me. Seriously! Why was I so devastated and what was the trigger?

God revealed to me that particular obsessions that we see from childhood could also be generational. Exploring this revelation, one day, I asked my mom why did she want to get married. As she shared her reasons, I remember the conversation eventually drifted to my grandmother, who never felt accepted or worthy because she had two children out of wedlock and never had a marriage.

Ashamed of her choices, my great grandmother sent my grandmother away when she became pregnant, and when she returned, my grandmother's children were never allowed to call her 'Mom'. My grandmother never received a higher level of education, her children were never allowed to call her mom and she never had a marriage. Although I believe she wanted to experience all of these things, she lived in a time where the mistakes she made, made her feel unworthy of any of these blessings. My mom saw the pain of her mom, raising two children as a single mother and was determined not to have the same fate. She made a promise to herself and God that she would wait until marriage to have sex, and she did. By 21, my mother was married, never having been touched by a man.

Although I never had children out of wedlock *(and it's only because Jesus was a fence during my many years of disobedience)*, my grandmothers' journey is much more similar to my own than my mother's journey. Being loved by a manmade my grandmother feel seen, accepted, loved, and validated. An existence without it felt like defeat. God needed me

6

to be aware that the struggles of our parents, grandparents, and sometimes great grandparents can also become our struggles. I believe my grandmother often felt defeated because she grew up in a time where people used marriage to validate you. I feel the pressure from never experiencing a union like this brought her a lot of pain and being unmarried, I shared her pain.

Some say there is nothing like being loved by the right person, and I'm not here to debate that. I think the more important lesson for my grandmother and I, is that a love like that from a human is the kind of love that could never complete you-- it's conditional, it can change. They can leave, change their minds or pass away, and while I hope a man can one day be a part of my life, he can never be my *entire* life. Life can't stop because it didn't turn out as I planned. I have to feel seen, accepted, loved, and validated before he ever arrives and every day after. This lie that my grandmother and I believed that we needed someone to "complete us" was a lie that had to stop with me! Generational curses are real, and it's up to us to break it off at the root.

Society's Expectations

I have read numerous articles that tell you that black educated women in their 30's are less likely to find a mate, and that the ratio of men to women is at an all-time low due to a significant amount of men already being married, in jail or gay, sending women into a frenzy that getting married is getting less likely to happen. Let's not forget that your biological clock is always ticking. No matter what it is, there is an angle that the media is pushing for you to believe that you're NOT worthy because a mate hasn't chosen you.

Whether we realize it or not, these reports play on our subconscious, it influences the things we daydream about and without knowing it, the desperation begins to play out in our lives. Have you ever met a guy you find extremely attractive or seen a photo of a guy you thought was cute or well put together? You start to imagine how your children would look, what kind of wedding you would have, and the lovely photos you will be able to post on social media? Yeah, sis, if that's you, that's crazy! I'm not saying this because I'm judging you-- ok I am-- but honestly it's because I have been this girl and I fight every day not to be her. Whether we know it or not, men can feel the desperation. This is why we have to be very aware of what we expose our self to, because the media will feed it to you!

Think about walking down an aisle of restaurants or different kiosks in the mall. When they run after you, anxiously trying to get you to listen to their sales pitch, 9 out of 10 times you continue to walk away. You didn't come in there looking for whatever it is they're trying to sell, so you walk right past them. However, have you ever walked past a high-end store? They're not beating the streets, begging you to come in. It's luxury. They have attained so much value, if you understand their worth, they know that you will come to them and if you don't they're ok with it. If you're not willing to do what it takes to obtain the value that they bring, they're okay with that. That's what you are sis. You are luxury; valuable. I don't care what society tries to tell you, you don't have to imagine what it would be like to be with him, to get him; sharpen your value, and your King will come to you.

I know it's irritating when people ask; Why aren't you married yet, like it's something I just happened to forget to do. We all know that marriage isn't as easy as going to the food store and grabbing some chicken. It's just not, but to be honest, I think most of these people mean well. So now I try not to get offended by their words, but I want us to realize what these words are doing to us subconsciously. Usain Bolt is known as the fastest man in the world. He has traveled the world with his gift, won numerous awards, and yet he still said in an interview that his mom often asks, "but when are you going to get married and give me some grandchildren?" Without even knowing it, a lot of us see marriage as the end-all-be-all, believing that our life only really begins when we get married, but it doesn't. So the next time someone is bold enough to ask, "Why aren't you married yet?" be strong enough to respectfully share this truth with them; *"there is more to life than obtaining a wedding ring."*

I've had the privilege to have conversations with many transparent married women, and on the days that are harder than others, it's their words that ring true in my ears. They have often told me that there is a whole other ball game of societal expectations, comparisons, and feelings of unfulfillment even after the ring. The pressure doesn't disappear after receiving the ring, so no matter what society may try to tell us, stand strong in this truth; a ring won't make us feel complete.

Lack of Trust

I once heard a Christian author say, "God wants you to get married more than you want to get married." This statement was so sobering. I couldn't understand how, if I have not been in a serious, committed relationship in almost seven years, how in the world could God want this for me, more than I wanted it for myself? Like Jesus couldn't possibly want this more than me, with all the praying and fasting I have already done.

When you're approaching your mid-thirties, this wait can often become overwhelming, and feel like you're doing something wrong? I've often heard the stories, "I placed my desire on my vision board, and God manifested my husband," "I prayed this prayer and months later he was here," "I heard a prophecy that he was on the way and the next week I met him." The thing about God is, you can do everything your friend did, have the same experiences and prophecies, but not one thing is going to happen before God's time. So if you're like me and you've done the vision boards, prayed the prayers and received the prophecies and you're still waiting, I want you to know that you are NOT alone.

When praying about these unfilled prayers and visions, I asked God, "if you want this for me more than I want it for myself how come I do not see it?" His answer was, 'surrender'. Surrender to the fact that your designed time for marriage may not be at the age of 21, 25, 32, or 35, it maybe 40, and that's still ok. My sorority sister got married for the first time a few months ago at the age of 62, so yes there is hope! We have to be willing to surrender to the fact that he may be shorter, younger, and less educated than we may have imagined, but it's going to be extremely purposeful. We may need to surrender that children may come later than we planned to have them or not at all, but we will have a life filled with love from our bonus children. God is saying the secret ingredient is to surrender.

I believe God wants to teach single women how to surrender now because I've heard that there is a whole lot more of it in marriage. A young girl that I mentor has expressed a lot of difficulties in her marriage to me, the constant pain she felt. She couldn't imagine that she would have to go through it. As an unmarried woman, I couldn't understand why she felt comfortable confiding in me, however, one of the things that I always tell her is to surrender it to God, because she can't humanly fix it or change her husband. We often want to do the fixing, and we can't. That's God's job. This is the advice God then told me to give to myself.

If we start to believe that my vision board, my prayer, or that person's prophecy manifested a spouse for me, we will continue to look to these things when things get hard in marriage. We can pray a million prayers, do several vision boards, and receive a whole heap of prophecies, but at the end of the day, God has the final say. I'm not saying we shouldn't pray, write the vision or receive the prophecies, but I want us to remember that God ordained long before you or I were in our mother's wombs, the appointed time that we would marry if it's in His will. Our job is to surrender and trust that although my process looks different from my neighbor's, God still knows best.

I was once watching a sermon entitled "Where is BAE?" *(slang for Before. Anyone. Else.)* I often avoided it, thinking, Lord, what kind of desperate title is this. However, Youtube kept recommending that I watch it, so I did. The premise of the sermon was enlightening but straightforward. "Bae is in the will of God." We would like to believe that we are often in the will of God, but when doing some soul searching, God revealed to me, that's not always the case.

As a hopeless romantic, I am indeed a sucker for "How We Met" stories. So when my friends are in new relationships, I often ask who, how, and when. I'm usually very intrigued by what kind of mind frame you were in before you met the person that would alter your universe forever. So when speaking with one of my friends about how she met her spouse, she expressed that during the process of surrendering her will to God a few months prior, that He revealed that she was a very negative person. So this was something she began to work on, merely having a more positive outlook on life in general. Within the next year of surrendering and becoming more positive, she bought a new home, got a raise at work, and met and began dating the man who she is now proud to call her husband.

Therefore not only is BAE in the will of God, every new blessing God has for us, starts with surrendering our will to Him and allowing Him to transform our minds so that we can see the opportunities with fresh eyes. This is key. When God asked me to be still and work on becoming more of who He has created me to be, I often got bored and frustrated spending more time praying, "So God, where is BAE?" than anything else. I then had to realize that "Seek ye first the kingdom of God" doesn't mean if we acknowledge that God exists, everything we want will fall into our lap. It means to trust God to be our everything and the blessings He has for our life will fall into place in His time.

The thing I realized about marriage is, if we want it bad enough, we can find a willing partner, bypass the tugging of God and get married. Like a lot of women I have had the opportunity to walk down the aisle a time or two, but I resisted because I knew the desire wasn't from God. I knew if couldn't learn how to trust God in my singleness by trying to control my desired destination, this behavior would most likely show up again in my marriage. I could just see myself trying to once again control the situation by continually finding new ways to change my husband, because once again things would have to go my way. However, I've heard countless stories of wives who say they have tried to change their spouse and it hasn't happened yet, because that's God's job. So when God asks us to trust His timing and surrender our timeline to Him, He is trying to prevent us from setting ourselves up for failure.

Fear of being Alone

A guy that I was once dating gave me such an excellent gift. At the time, I didn't realize his words were actual gifts, but after a time of reflection, I realized how much these statements undoubtedly shaped my life. One of the things he told me was, " You need to learn how to enjoy being by yourself." At the time, I was confused! Learn to be by myself? Why? I didn't see any sense in this statement. We were seriously dating, we would soon be married (in my mind at least), and I would never have to be by myself again, so why was this a trait I needed to learn * blank stare*. Little did I know, my plan wasn't his plan, nor was it God's plan. Even if it was, would I still need to learn to by myself? Yup! I would!

What I realized is that a lot of us want to get married so that we will no longer have to be alone. Those R&B songs in the nineties set us up for failure! But seriously, I had no idea how valuable alone time was. When we're alone is when God reveals His most powerful words to us. While I was alone, I found my gift of writing. While I was alone, I found myself. What this guy was trying to tell me is that 'you are so eager to attach yourself to me when you haven't even spent any time with you'. That's scary. If we're not whole before we get married, we will drain everything out of that human, with unrealistic expectations.

When I am alone, I'm restored by God from worries of the day. I begin to reflect on the visions and goals God has given me. When I desired to be in the company of a mate, I wanted him to restore me, encourage me, and help me plan out our next steps. I told myself that I wasn't good enough on my own, so I wanted someone on this journey with me. My dysfunctional behavior led to the second statement he said to me years later, "I don't think I could marry you because you're too selfish."

Boy, did this statement hit me like a ton of bricks! "Too selfish". These words were hard to accept because I did the "girlfriend duties". You know; encourage you when you're down, support your goals and dreams and accompany you to the things you would like to do.

However, those were duties that I did once it was convenient for me. Making a sacrifice to put someone's desires and concerns above yours when there is something you want to do more than anything is when you're self-less. I'm currently reading a life-changing book written by a couple married for over 40 years; it's called "The Meaning of Marriage." In-depth, they explain that the secret of marriage is to understand that it's the replica of Christ's love for the church. You are consistently putting the other person's needs above your own, even when they don't deserve it.

Without the help of the Spirit, without a continual refilling of your soul's tank with the glory and love of the Lord, such submission to the interest of others is virtually impossible to accomplish for any length of time without becoming resentful. You can only afford to be generous if you have money in the bank to give. In the same way, if your only source of love and meaning is your spouse then anything they fail to do, will cause you grief and you will have no way to refill your love tank.

If I had gotten married in my 20's this would have been my reality, no doubt about it. I expected him to fulfill my needs. My self-worth was wrapped up in a relationship and even when it wasn't, simply expecting that he would always put me first and always get it right, was not a reflection of our relationship with Christ. We fall short of God's glory every day, and he loves us just the same. Queen, your future husband or your now husband cannot be the only source of your love tank, because there will be many days it will run empty, and he won't be able to fill it up. Only God truly fills our insecurities and inadequacies.

Many things can keep us in a state of longing for a title that may or may never arrive. Generational Roots, Society, Lack of Trust and Fear of being alone are just some of the things I had to break free of to understand the truth of who God created me to be. However, we can't wallow in the things that have contributed to our feelings of unworthiness. We must be aware of them so that we can recognize our triggers in our moments of weakness. I believe it's natural to desire marriage and to share a life with someone but our motives must always be pure. Is our desire coming from a broken place, and can we still trust God if He ever says, "this is not in the good and perfect plan I've set for you"? Knowing that God's plans are different from our own may be a hard pill to swallow, but it may be the reality for some of us, and we have to trust that God knows best.

For a lot of us, marriage has been a lifetime goal, and some of you reading this may have "achieved" this goal, but if you're honest, being married isn't enough to fulfill you for the rest of your life. The honeymoon phase may be significant, but you know there is more that God has called you to do. Society will remind you of it too, and they don't let the ink dry on your wedding certificate before they start asking about when you're going to have kids. If we're not careful, we can make marriage feel like a box checked. Soon enough, your spouse won't be enough, the person you once longed for now tossed to the side as you strive for another goal, because you realize marriage wasn't the "big" thing you were missing. There was more, whether your more is a home, a kid or thriving careers, marriage alone won't be enough!

Put on Your Crown

We teach people how to treat us. So if someone meets me in a desperate state, a state where I need this relationship more than anything, He will know that without him I don't feel worthy. Queen, God wanted me to tell you that with or without the title of wife or "Mrs." your title of Queen has always been there. Don't forget to wear it with pride, and don't toss it aside out of the desperation of wanting to own the other titles. You've always been royalty. **1 Peter 2:9 NIV** *"But you are a chosen people, a royal priesthood, a holy nation, God's possession that you may declare the praises of him who called you out of darkness into his wonderful light."*

When I accepted Christ, I became a part of His royal family. So ladies, I sometimes have to remind myself *(and I hope that this is a reminder to you, too)* let's not be defined by the finder, but first be crowned by the sender, which is Christ. The Bible also says in **Proverbs 18:22 NIV**, *"He that finds a wife finds a good thing and obtains favor from the Lord."* and as many pastors have translated, "you're a wife before he finds you." When we accept Christ and become apart of his family, He loves us like his bride. **Ephesians 22: 25 NIV** *"Husbands love your wives, as Christ loves the church and gave himself up for her."* God already showed you how you were created to be loved, so ladies let's remember that we are the good thing!

Myles Munroe was a man who knew the worth of his wife, his good thing. In one of his interviews he said everywhere he went, he had a book present: in the bathroom, his office, his car, he always wanted to be engrossed in a chapter so that he was still learning. Then he said that his wife reads way more than him! In a sense he was saying, that if you think I am wise or insightful, you should meet my wife, as her appetite for learning is even greater than my own.

A lot of times after people find out that I'm single, they ask me the question, "So why are you still single?" This statement by Myles Munroe has a lot to do with it, and I'll tell you why. If you've ever played the game of chess, you will know while the King is an essential piece, the Queen is the most powerful. I haven't met a man that truly understands the value that I bring to the game as a Queen. This is also because, for a long time, I didn't understand my worth.

Now that I do, I understand that I must choose wisely because of the game I was designed to play. You see in life, and in chess, your Queen helps you navigate your path, she protects you, covers you, and grows with you.

This is what Myles Munroe's wife did for him. We all know him as this amazing international preacher and thought leader. However what he was saying with the above statement that his wife reads more than him, is that he wouldn't be the man he was today, if he didn't partner in life with a woman who had an appetite for learning as much as his wife did.

Like Mrs. Munroe; I think different, I dream different, and I grow different. I was designed to protect a King, not a pawn, and so were you. Know your worth as a Queen.

God has already called us Queens. He's just waiting for us to receive the crown.

♥ CRACK THE CODE:

1. Why do/did you want to get married?

2. What if you never get married? Would you be mad at God?

3. Married Queens: Do you ever blame your husband for your marriage not being everything you thought it would be? What has God revealed to you about this concern?

♛ QUEEN HACKS:

> I found that loneliness hits me more when I'm idle so I tend to schedule out my life (details in chapter 12 on how) to make sure I keep my time occupied not just with random things but with activities that align with what I value and also help me to grow! E.g., I try to read at least 30 minutes every day, this helps me keep my attention on something that is productive and evidently helps me to grow.

> Take social media breaks; it helps to kill comparison. The more you compare your lack of love or current love life to others, the more you will seek complete fulfillment in it. Remember married or not, a man can never completely fulfill you!

CHAPTER 2

IF IT ISN'T PURPOSE, IT'S POINTLESS

Many are the plans in a person's heart,
but it is the Lord's purpose that prevails
Proverbs 19:21 NIV

I met Devon Franklin and Meagan Good in 2013 when they came to the Bahamas for a conference, where I served as the head of marketing. This conference was the first time I met him and it was at that moment that I decided to informally pitch my idea to turn my play *Sarah's Wedding* into a movie. I knew it would probably be nothing but a seed, and that's exactly what happened, a seed was planted. Two years later, when I moved to LA to take up a screenwriter course, he agreed to meet me at Sony studios. I was so excited, I made the Uber drop me there an hour early to ensure I would be on time. I spent countless hours working on a pitch and drawing up a powerpoint so that I could make a formal pitch to him to begin working on my movie. I had rave reviews about *Sarah's Wedding* and everyone told me if you get to pitch this to a Hollywood Executive I know someone will want to make it into a movie.

So I went into the meeting, said my greetings, and began my pitch. Midway Devon stopped me and told me that I had a lot more growing to do before I could deliver a pitch and have a Hollywood producer pick it up. Talk about EMBARRASSED! I had spent the last few months studying screenwriting, and I thought this was my moment. Even though they told us in our screenwriting classes that getting discovered in this way was next to impossible, I still believed I had a shot. I didn't even get to pull out my powerpoint before he explained that he granted the meeting to give me some encouragement and some direction on my journey, but working with him at this point was not going to be an option. I was crushed! The meeting must have lasted 20 minutes before he sent me on my way with a screenwriting book he recommended along with an encouragement to do more writing and take some more classes. My opportunity of a lifetime turned into a book recommendation and a pat on the back, but even though I couldn't see it then, his rejection was simply redirection.

Confused about what my next step was going to be in LA, I kept trying to work on my talent visa. I had spent over three grand on lawyer fees, and my money was running low. I remember the exact moment I knew it was time to return home. I was sitting at brunch with a group of black female TV writers feeling super posh when the waiter came up to me and said, "I'm sorry, ma'am, the machine declined your card." Utterly embarrassed, and wondering why he couldn't whisper in my ear, I handed him another card and prayed like nobody's business. Following your dreams to Hollywood is already hard when you're an actual American citizen. As an immigrant who can't legally work, you're just paying bills with absolutely no income. The signs were on the wall loud and clear: it was time to go home. However, I was determined to return, so I left some of my luggage promising the family friend that I lived with and all of my friends that I would be back once the summer was over. When I lived in LA I was going to private book releases hosted by Mary Shriver, riding escalators with Meagan Good and taking selfies with Sarah Jakes Roberts, I thought; "I'm living my best life," but God had other plans for me. I never went back, and I never finished my talent visa application. Why not, you ask?

After my summer home, I didn't earn nearly as much money as I thought I would make to return to LA in the Fall. I started to wrack my brain about how I would afford to return, and I heard God say "you're not going" "I'm sorry, what?" I replied. I had already invested over three thousand dollars in lawyer fees for my talent visa. I had to go back, I had to keep trying! God asked me if I wanted to lose three thousand more dollars. That's the day I learned who the boss was!

I moved to LA a few weeks after I released my first book, weeks after I had told the world through my words that the love thing didn't quite work out for me, so watch out Hollywood here I come. I thought I had my whole career journey ahead of me, only to find out a couple of months later, I had to move back. Desperate to feel worthy, significant, and seen I wanted to prove to the world that I may not have gotten the guy, but I'm making waves in my career.

God allowed me to gain the knowledge, and then He started slowly stripping things away until I realized that season was over for me. See, the man looks at the outward appearance, but God looks at the heart. T.D. Jakes once preached a sermon warning us to watch the seeds of our dreams. So many of us are making empires based on the lie that we're not good enough. Wanting to prove to that ex-boyfriend, ex-husband, or family member that even though they left, you're still winning!

So why do we do it? Why do some of us chase a career with so much enthusiasm, when it may not even be a part of God's plan for us?

I got a BIG Ego!

We've heard the concept that if we really want something we have to be willing to do the work, but the question is at what cost? What are we putting at risk when we become obsessed with this journey of climbing the corporate ladder? Have you ever met those women who look in disdain at the women who have always dreamed about their wedding day? With assurance they admit, that's never been an issue for me; I didn't grow up thinking about those things. However, what I want to tell you is, just because your obsession is different than hers, it doesn't make you better, it just makes you different. At the end of the day, like the anxious bride-to-be, your hunger and thirst may still be built on something that will never sustain you.

So, why do some of us make our career our life's obsession, to the point that we're willing to risk it all to make our dreams a reality? For a lot of us, it's an ego trip. We want people to associate us with what we were able to do with all our hard work. It's the mentality that 'I built this, I made this happen, I worked my butt off, and now I'm enjoying the fruits of my labor.' No matter how hard we work, God will always seek to remind us that it's His divine alignment that brings forth the successful milestones in our career.

One of my favorite podcasts, *How I Built This* by Guy Raz, features interviews of famous entrepreneurs that share the companies they built and how they made them. Companies like Airbnb, Instagram, Spanx, and BET, to name a few. I love to hear the stories of their journey to greatness, and at the end of every interview, there is ONE question he asks every guest. How much of what you built you feel is attributed to your hard work? How much is due to luck, and often most of the guests say 'both'. Now I don't believe in luck or coincidence, so it warms my heart when I hear some guests say, "I do think it's both, but I don't call it luck. I call it a blessing or an ordained connection from God". Either way, they have realized that although I hustle and I hustle hard, all of this that is currently around me, could never just be me.

It's crazy how God sometimes uses our hustle and other times the "lack" of a hustle to propel us forward. A lot of us think God blessing us looks like success, or prosperity. But what happens when He says success looks like scaling back?

One of my current favorite preachers Michael Todd, seemed as if he blew up overnight. So when a Youtuber released a video on "Who is Michael Todd?*" I was curious to know what was it that turned him into this seemingly overnight success.

In the video, he shared, that the year before the world knew his name, God told him to cancel his church's annual Christmas production. This

20

production was what brought in most of their members every year, so how could he cancel? But God told him to pull back. I want you to know in every definition of the word Pastor Todd considers himself a hustler. So when God said don't network, don't put on a Christmas production and obey my steps, this was a very hard thing for him to do.

A lot of times to the human eyes, we feel if we're not hustling, then we're losing. Still, that same Christmas that Pastor Todd canceled his Christmas production, God had a random young lady that Pastor Todd has never met, cut up one of his clips from a series he did earlier that year on "Relationship Goals" and posted it on Twitter. In less than 48 hours, this clip had received over two million views. He had been releasing sermons on his Youtube page for well over three years, and in about a month after this particular post, his subscription list went from 1800 to 180,000. He could have never "hustled" this growth. He knew it could only be God. Pastor Todd said God told him, "You don't need what you think you need for what I'm going to do."

When God is driving the ship, you're not going to get the credit. Pastor Todd reminded us that when God is asking us to do less, it's because He wants us to recognize what it looks like when He does more. Hustling doesn't always lead to a reward, but trusting God always will.

Identity

I remember one time someone was trying to describe to me a lady to me and one of the first descriptions after her name was, "she's a lawyer." Growing up on an island, a career like Doctor, Lawyer, or Engineer still carry a lot of weight. You can have the most outgoing personality, a giving heart, or make a mean sweet potato pie, but nine times out of ten, most people will describe you by your profession.

If you grew up in a house or a community that praised specific careers and refused to fund the dreams of others, whether you followed the status quo or rebelled and followed your own goals, there is a high chance your profession can become your identity. People ask you more often, "What do you do for a living?" versus "Who are you?"

I can almost guarantee if I ask someone, "Who are you?" They would be taken aback as to why I was asking such a profound question.

Kobe Bryant once said in an interview that he would rather be remembered for jump-starting tech companies than his skills on the court.* When asked about this bold statement, he replied, "I believe that we must always challenge ourselves to evolve and grow." He said it's because he never wants to lose himself in his career. Kobe went on to say that it's tough for athletes not to attach their identity to what they do and not who they are, and that's a very hazardous zone. He shared that you should always be trying to go after the next stage of your life with the same intensity, the same attention to details the same tenacity, and you can't do this if you're obsessed with making your career your identity.

If Kobe Bryant, one of the best basketball players who ever lived, doesn't only want to be remembered or known as just a basketball player, why do we spend so much of our lives in pursuit of finding our identity through our career? This short moment of clarity is why famous athletes like Kobe went on to do more. I believe Oprah is known for more than just the Oprah Winfrey Show, and Rhianna is no longer just a pop singer from Barbados because they all understood that who they are was more significant than what they did as a career.

I Trust My Career, More than I Trust God

I entered the corporate world after almost nine years in the public education system. That's the day I officially became a "Girl Boss." I had moved to the capital (Nassau, Bahamas), had my apartment, and was living the "good life." However, six months into my "Who Run the World" soundtrack, 90% of employees at the company I worked for were made redundant. Hold up, my career was supposed to be a source of strength, the thing that kept me going! How after only six months, was it being pulled from under me?

Confused about what was next after God said not to go back to a 9-5, I went back and forth with the idea of going into mission work and going to LA to enroll in a screenwriting curriculum. This was the season when I chose to go to LA, and even though I still believe LA was a part of the road I was meant to travel, the timing of it all was God's plan.

For the last four years, I have been on the unpredictable road of entrepreneurship. I think if you ever want to understand what it means to surrender entirely to God, you should become an entrepreneur. This road has been confusing, depressing, and overwhelming but worth every second. It's crazy how the hardest times of our lives can become the most rewarding. Entrepreneurship is truly a calling because when you think you hold the cards, something else happens that seeks to throw you off your game.

Social media tends to put us in a craze of trying to be as "successful" as another person, who has an entirely different story than we do. We grew up in a world where media makes us believe "we can have it all," so this is what we strive for. Regardless of God's direction in our life we want to make it happen, but Michelle Obama said it best when she said, "we can have it all, just not all at the same time." We must also remember that the problem with trying to have it all is that it sometimes comes at the expense of doing the things God has called us to do.

God made me take a more in-depth look at myself because He is the boss. And I needed to know that to the world, I'm not always going to look like a "Girl Boss." One of my steady forms of income for the last four years has been private swimming lessons. I run from a glamorous speaking engagement to throwing on a swim cap and jumping into a pool, as this is a source of income that's helped keep me stable over the last few years. When I'm wet and driving to another location, I ask God, "What is your plan? I used to be working with an international company that sent me away on training, gave me a cell phone, and invited me to private VIP events, I liked my corporate job! God this entrepreneurial life has me confused, what's the meaning behind riding around in this wet T-shirt, and where is this start-up company going?"

He reminded me that there is a purpose in every season and that this season is simply preparation for the next one, I had to learn to trust Him and not the job. I thought the one good thing about being an entrepreneur is that you no longer have to worry about someone telling you what to do. I felt despite the challenges, you were officially the boss. However, when we accept Jesus Christ as our savior, whether we work for ourselves or the corporate world, He will always have the final say. I tried for years to leave the education system, and God kept saying not yet! After I became an entrepreneur, my old corporate job, called me back three times for an interview, a job I would have killed for years before, offered me countless opportunities, and I had to turn them down because God was calling me to more. Not more money at the time, but more of an impact.

When I look at the countless entrepreneurs that started their companies after that company went through that massive termination, it makes me think that this unfortunate circumstance was the exact push we needed to push us into purpose. Not because I believe entrepreneurship is the only way to explore purpose, but because we stepped out on faith when we felt like we had no other choice.

Listen I get it, it's hard to walk away from a job that pays well and has great benefits, but the reason it's hard is because we're scared if we take the leap of faith and walk away we won't be able to survive or feed our families. However hanging on to a job for dear life only because you believe it will always sustain you, doesn't prevent them from one day sending you an email and pulling the entire rug out from under you. If there is another company God has been leading you to, don't ignore Him, He will sustain you. If it's a nonprofit he wants you to join or start, keep your ear to the ground, He will open the doors. **Psalm 20:7 NIV** *Some trust in chariots and some in horses, but we trust in the name of the Lord our God.*

A lot of us modern women struggle with making our careers the center of our lives. Some of us do it for the recognition, we want to stroke our own ego, some of us make it our entire identity; placing our self worth in our career and some of us use it as our safety net and source of strength.

That's why it's so vital that we continually check our motives for achievements and never forget to acknowledge who is the actual boss; Christ. God knew if He allowed me to get my movie made when I first moved to LA my ego most likely couldn't handle it and I would have begun to trust more what a Hollywood producer could do for me rather than what God wanted to do through me. I honestly don't always understand the journey God is taking me on but I remain thankful for it. Even though it would be so much easier to choose a profession based on the world's standards, if it's not purpose, my heart simply can't connect to it.

💡 CRACK THE CODE:

1. What would you say if someone were to ask, Who are you outside of your career?

2. Have you ever struggled with making your career your identity, being hungry for recognition, or tried to use it to fulfill insecurity? If so, how did you overcome it? If still struggling, evaluate the source of this motive.

👑 QUEEN HACKS:

> Watch Simon Sinek's TED Talk - *Start with Why* and evaluate if your current work-life aligns with your why

> Put the *Purpose Driven Life* by Rick Warren on your reading list

CHAPTER 3

WAITING ON YOUR WOMB

"I am learning to trust the journey even when I do not understand it"

- Mila Bron

Most things we have a strong desire for in life, if we wanted it, we could honestly bypass God's will and make them happen for ourselves. Marriage, Money, or Fame-- if we wanted these things bad enough, we could manipulate situations to manifest these things in our life except giving birth to a child. The timing of this miracle is determined only by God.

No matter the number of times we have sex or go through in vitro, when it comes to bringing a new life into the world, God has the final say. Accepting that we don't always have control over a situation is often disheartening when, for the most part, we like to think that we have some form of control over what we do and what happens in our lives. Especially today, we are a generation of, "We want what we want, and we want it now." And for the most part, we can get it. However, what happens when the thing you want more than anything doesn't happen as you planned?

Like most young girls, starting a family was also a big deal on my list of life achievements, so much so that I kept myself in a job I hated, only because it would be an excellent job for a "Mom." I wasn't even married, yet here I was placing my purpose on pause for something that I hoped would happen. I stayed in the perfect job for a family without having a family. Heck, I'm still not married and I left that job five years ago.

The thing is, most women dream about one day having a family, and there is nothing wrong with that. I truly believe having a desire to have a family and children of your own is a natural and great desire for your life. However, I think the problem arises when we as women decide that we want a family more than we want God's will for our lives. Take a moment and reflect on the following questions and answer them honestly for yourself.

If you never become a Mom, would you stop trusting God?

Do you feel your life still has purpose, without the title of Mom?

Do you need to birth a legacy to view yourself as a Queen?

If you are someone who has longed for a child, when you see cute kids, you touch your stomach and say, "Oh my ovaries!" Have you ever asked yourself, "Why do I want a child" ? Your motives may indeed be pure, but I think it's always worth exploring why we have such a strong desire for motherhood. I'll admit I have often said I want to give my parents grandbabies. I always knew my dad wanted grandbabies, so that was one of the reasons I kept hoping it would happen for me. As I got older, I was open to marrying a guy with kids, because it removed the pressure if I wasn't able to have any for my husband. Of course, I want kids, too, and I would love to raise children in the fear and admonition of God, but if I'm honest, some of my desires also had to do with fulfilling that need for someone else.

The Holy Spirit reminded me of Romans 12:1, which reads, "Brothers and sisters, since God has shown us great mercy, I beg you to offer your lives as a living sacrifice to him. Your offering must be only for God and pleasing to him."

This verse reminds me that my focus should be on filling the needs and desires of God alone. It's about what God wants for our lives, however, as humans, we carry the weight and pressure of others when hoping and planning to give birth to a child. So many women are crippled with pain, feeling like a failure because of outside pressures. Sis, it's not worth it, if this is your struggle, know that no matter how much anyone around you may want you to have a child, God's timing is still the best!

I think it's so important that we take an honest inventory of our motives. I honestly want us to take a minute together to take an inventory of our heart and why we desire, or desired children:

I will feel fulfilled and complete when I have a child

I believe tradition and society has unconsciously made a lot of us feel, that our life has finally reached a level of fulfillment when we have created a family. I don't believe this is true. Don't believe me? Ask any mother you know! Shoot, ask your mother if she stopped having desires or longings in life once she became a mother. I think that the majority of their responses will be no, because as humans we are designed to keep growing. Our areas for fulfillment will often shift into a new space.

I remember talking with an acquaintance as she approached her 30th birthday. Now for some women turning 30 can be daunting, and I get it, it's because some of us at 30 haven't "accomplished" the things our parents did at 30. We may or may not be a little more educated, but as far as traditional goals, a lot of us have not obtained degrees, gotten married, become parents, and homeowners all before the age of 30, which my parents were.

However, this young lady had done quite a bit. By 30, she had become a certified public accountant. She was serving as a financial controller for a very prominent company. She was married with three kids and was actively serving in her church. So for me, she was killing it for 30. Yet as she approached that number, she began feeling depressed, thinking that there was so much more she wanted to accomplish but hadn't achieved yet. I was utterly confused, like what else do you want? I know so many women who wished their resumes were similar to hers by the age of 30. So one day, while we were having lunch, I asked her, "What in the world could you possibly be depressed about?"

She said that being a homeowner was something she thought she would have accomplished by now, along with having the opportunity to travel like she had seen so many peers her age do. I spent so much time idolizing women who had the opportunity to start their families before their biological clock kicked in, not realizing the sacrifices they had to make and the strong desires that still played against their insecurities, fears, and doubts. She thought the void was due to being able to travel and own a home, however I believe until we allow God to fill that void, we are always going to be seeking more. Without Him we are just transferring the pain to another bandaid.

What I want us to realize as women is, that the longing in the pit in your stomach that cries every time a friend announces a pregnancy date, has a gender reveal party or posts maternity photos is about more than a desire for a baby. The more we focus on the things we lack, the less we will see greatness within us. The enemy has led us to believe that the missing piece is earthly, and as long as the enemy can make you think that he can keep you distracted from the fullness of Christ. Your longing is for Christ.

I remember praying for years with a friend for her and her husband to give birth to their first child. Years after constant tears and prayers, God blessed her womb. However, the baby didn't make it. A year later, God once again blessed her womb. We were so excited! We were standing and basking in the joy of an answered prayer. A few months later, she felt torn between the pleasure of caring for her newborn and the passing months of unemployment. She didn't mind too much being out of work during his first three months, but by the time six months hit, she was once again battling depression. They had a mortgage, a kid to feed, future school fees, and were living on one salary. How long would they have to endure this trying season?

One day I messaged her and told her to give it to God. Her dilemma wasn't Christ's first rodeo. For years we prayed and waited for the miracle standing right in front of her. And although motherhood was everything she dreamed of and more, being a mother now also brought other concerns and desires. Desires, she had to once again surrender to God. She began to make an effort to enjoy the blessing sitting in front of her and leave the financial burden to God. After a little over six months, and she got a call for an interview. She got a job!

In the interview, God reminded her of a prayer she prayed years before she ever got pregnant. She didn't want to only have three months off like most Bahamian mothers have when they have a child, she wanted to spend at least six months with her child after the child was born. God wasn't just making her wait, He answered a prayer. Her life wasn't complete once she had a child, because having a child brought on new insecurities, being able to financially provide for her child now became the focus of feeling complete.

I'm pretty sure this isn't the first time you heard that your life wouldn't automatically be perfectly fulfilled once you have a child. So why do we still secretly feel that once it does happen we will be content? The answer is trust. We trust the social media photos that show the happy faces of family and friends who have seen this dream come true. We believe in the 'seen' more than the 'unseen'. So no matter how many times God tells us that the longing in the pit of our stomach is for Him, we have convinced ourselves that it is due to this unfulfilled dream. I want to remind you that it isn't! It's a mirage.

Feel Less Than a Woman

I've never personally gone through the journey of actively trying to conceive a child. However, I have watched and joined in prayer with many friends who have struggled with this level of disappointment. We spent so many years in our late teens and early 20's doing everything possible NOT to get pregnant, it's ironic how hard it is now. A lot of women find themselves actively trying to get pregnant, and still, nothing happens.

I watched one of my friends share her journey of the heartbreak of losing a child one night and one thing stood out to me as she walked us through the journey of her miscarriage. She said she felt like less than a woman when her body couldn't carry her baby to full term. At the time, she didn't realize how difficult it was to conceive, nor how common miscarriages are. She said during her miscarriage was the first time her mom ever shared with her that she too had a miscarriage in the past.

According to yourfertility.org the chances of a couple getting pregnant on any given month are 10- 30%, and this percentage decreases in your 30's. Ladies, this is not to discourage you, it's to reassure you that it doesn't make you less of a woman when you don't get pregnant. As all women face these percentages, It's honestly nothing but a faith walk and if God has designed this as apart of your future he can and will bring it to pass.

We have to know that being able to have a child naturally won't prove that we are women. There is nothing wrong with how God made you, you were made in His image, specially crafted for the purpose He has for your life. You're not missing the "mother gene" just because you haven't conceived. I've met so many older women who love children and are very nurturing to their nieces, nephews, and the children of their church, yet God didn't have it in His plan to bless them with a child.

So often, the question is 'why'? Why would God make me a woman with the desire to conceive and raise children in this world and not grant this wish? The answer is, "I don't know" His ways are past finding out. **Romans 11:33 NIV** - *Oh, the depth of the riches of the wisdom and knowledge of God! How unsearchable his judgments, and his paths beyond tracing out!* What I do know is that there is a purpose in your pain. There is someone who you are meant to reach with your testimony. Some lives will change because of your motherly instinct and longing to connect with children. God is sovereign, and the last thing He intended when He set you on this journey was for you to feel unworthy.

In an interview with Dwayne Wade and Gabrielle Union, they shared with Oprah their journey to becoming parents. During the interview, Dwayne shared he was starting to get worried about Gabrielle's health because there were so many things she was doing to her body to bring forth a child that after a while, he told her it wasn't worth it. He wanted a child with her, just as much as she wanted it, but no child would ever be worth risking her life.

One of the gifts of being a woman involves an excellent opportunity to bring a child into this world. For some people, it seems like it comes so easily. So as I watched several friends and family members pain with wanting for this experience to naturally happen for them, I can't help but ask God why? The truth is, God knew us before we were in our mother's womb. He knew what our bodies would bring forth and what are bodies would reject. Our experiences shape us into the blessings we will be for others. We were born into a life of sin, and Christ died so that we may have life and have it more abundantly. So even when that abundance doesn't look the way we imagined it, know that God is still working it out for our good.

Leaving a legacy

A lot of us have want children or grandchildren because we want to leave a legacy on this earth. I know this feeling all too well, and while I understand it, this is also another motive we have to surrender to Christ. The first reason being that if God can do anything, and if He wanted me to have the child, as long as I was doing everything physically possible to procreate, the child would be here. So if we feel that there is a tug from God about leaving our legacy, we must believe that He will do it. God can do it through childbirth in the right season or through the lives you touch through your nieces, nephews, godchildren, bonus children, or adopted ones. But no matter what, it will be well done. When my brother passed away, I was shocked at the many friends he had, who expressed that their child would miss their Uncle Kenny. Here I was crying about how he never had kids of his own or had the opportunity to be a biological Uncle through my sister or me, when biology didn't really matter, because there were so many loved children who knew him as their Uncle Kenny. His legacy will continue to live on through the hearts he touched, including his adopted nieces and nephews.

Queen, your legacy doesn't have to be remembered only through your biological children. It's more about the lives you had the chance to touch along the way. So if you're sitting home moping and not surrounding yourself with the community because you can't believe God won't bless your womb, you're missing out on a million opportunities to leave a legacy. I remember interviewing an artist who was 'getting up there' in age and still not married. I asked him if he wasn't interested in getting married and having kids. He replied, "for what?" I said, "I don't know to leave a legacy?" At that time, this was one of the top reasons on my list. He then said to me, "I already have kids. I birthed my paintings; they are my legacy. Whenever I die, they will live on in memory of me". The thing is, he was right. Long after he leaves the earth, his paintings will still be here. This is a reminder to trust God with your path. Trust when His ways don't look like our ways. Care about His will, more than you care about how he is writing your legacy.

A Two person family doesn't feel like a Gift

Just like singleness is a gift, I also believe the time you have with just you and your husband is also a gift. I remember having a conversation with a young lady who told me she had been married for several years but hadn't had children yet. Like a lot of insensitive people, I asked the question that a lot of women aren't ready for or want to deal with; "So why don't you have kids yet?" If you are reading this and you are in this season, please forgive my ignorance. Thankfully she didn't get upset, she just smiled and said, "Because we don't want them yet".

She wanted to use this time to continue to learn and enjoy her husband, along with taking moments to chase her career with vigor and commitment. Although she wished to have children eventually, she understood that this season, where she and her husband could come and go as they please and travel with just the two of them, was rare. She was soaking in every moment of that experience and trusted that if it were God's will to have a child, they one day would, but as for now, she was living in that beautiful moment.

Years later, she gave birth to an amazing little boy, but that day her statement sobered me. In whatever state she was, she learned how to be content. Yes, it was also her decision to wait, but I admired that she knew that this time with her and her husband was a beautiful season that should be enjoyed.

Today as you read this chapter, I want to ask you to say a silent prayer for those women who struggle with the wait, and if that's you, include your fears, desires, and anxiety too. Know that God has the power to bring everything to fruition that He has promised you, but even more importantly, know that He has already given you the greatest gift He could ever have given you. He calls you Queen!

💡 CRACK THE CODE:

1. What do you like or would love to do, but couldn't do at all or as much if you had children? Do it now!! If it's becoming an entrepreneur, traveling, being faithful in the gym, or joining a book club, whatever it is, make a list of at least five things you could be doing and take steps toward starting at least one today!

2. Meditate on the story of Hannah in 1 Samuel Chapter 1 and ask God to reveal to you what He wants you to learn or know more about during this trying season.

👑 QUEEN HACKS:

> Babysit a niece or nephew or one of your friends' kids! I did this for the first time a short time ago and realized that it was the first time I ever changed a diaper, made a bottle or bathed a child! Don't judge me, I'm

the last child with no nieces or nephews! The point is, this gave me some experience, it also made me tired (I came home every night wanting to write and never did). Build on these moments, they're golden.

> Mentor someone who isn't a family member or a friend's child. I filled my longings by helping to groom young lives through mentorship. There is something special about having the chance to affect change in someone's life not out of obligation because we're related, but simply because I want to help you grow. Church youth groups, community organizations, and/or orphanages that may be looking for mentors are great places to start.

CHAPTER 4

MONEY, POWER & FAME

I think everybody should get rich and famous and do everything
they ever dreamed of so they can see that it's not the answer.

- Jim Carrey

The world teaches us that the more we have, the more successful we are. When I went to Greece, I met a missionary family where both of their incomes came from the mercies of what people committed or felt led to give every year. Before becoming a missionary, the father worked a high paying job with luxuries and benefits, including his apartment. When he decided to become a missionary, he surrendered all of the comforts that he once knew in obedience to God's will for his life. Observing their life and choices, it reminded me of a quote that I heard, "Success isn't about the number of things that we collect, but as Christians, our progress depends on our obedience to God". To the world, this couple's "social status" would be seen as middle to low income, but to God, they are worth so much more.

I think the reason so many of us struggle with wanting to obtain the version of success that looks like unlimited money, fame, and power is because we aren't performing for an audience of one. We have forgotten that when we choose Christ, we decided to lay our life down for His.

Now, I'm not saying that I believe that as Christians, all of us should sell all of our items and live like nomads on the street preaching the gospel. I just want us to challenge our motives. Is money is our source of happiness or is it a tool we use to affect change? We all have to answer that question honestly for ourselves. I do NOT believe money is the root of all evil, but I do think the *love* of money is the root of all evil. **1 Timothy 6:10** – *"For the love of money is a root of all kinds of evil. Some people, eager for money, have wandered from the faith and pierced themselves with many griefs."*

I once was in a Christian finance seminar where Michael Pittman said, that people like to mention all the time, "Money can't buy happiness". He challenged people to realize that they looked at this statement selfishly: They assume that the person that they can try to make happy with this money is themselves. However, when your payment is used to bless others, it can bring happiness. He referenced the students from Morehouse College who all got their tuition loans paid for at graduation, everyone in the room had to admit that all of these men were pretty happy. So in a sense, money can buy happiness. If we're honest though, when the majority of us think about making money, it's not because we want to give 90% of it away, it's because we want the money for ourselves. Including me!

So lets honestly explore the reasons why we feel that once we obtain more money, fame, or power, we will finally be happy.

Financial Freedom

One of the reasons I believe a lot of us want to obtain wealth is the freedom that wealth gives us to do whatever we want. I have to admit that financial freedom feels good. I side hustled by teaching swimming to be able to afford some of my travel ventures, and it felt good when I was able to purchase a ticket to go. I didn't have to ask anyone for a loan, I had the freedom to decide to go.

However, even though it feels good when we want to get something done and have the money to do it, how many of us actually stop to pray about a purchase or decision when we already have the money? When you don't have the money you make yourself open for God to bless you.

I remember the first time I heard, transformational speaker and life coach, Lisa Nichols was coming to the Bahamas. I knew she was worth the seventy-five dollar ticket, however, I did not have it. So I began to pray about how to best approach the situation and my answer lead me to be more resourceful. I know that I had excellent skills when it comes to event planning and production management, so I called the organizer and offered my services free of charge. These services were worth ten times the price of the ticket. However, serving Lisa Nichols for 48 hours would be priceless. The organizer initially replied that she didn't need my services and that she had a full team that was able to handle the workload. I was devastated, but I knew God would provide an opportunity for me to see her.

A few weeks later, the organizer called back and said that she could use my help after all! I was super excited. God had opened the door! I would be able to get one on one time serving someone I deeply admired and wouldn't have to spend a dime! I had been resourceful, and it had paved the way. Then God asked me to sponsor a young woman from my church to go to the conference. I was confused. I had used my resources to get myself a free experience, and now I was going to have to sponsor someone else. However, I was obedient, having NO clue where the money for her ticket was going to come from, God made me write in my journal a commitment to buy the ticket. Thirty minutes later, I went to a swim class where I was going to make twenty dollars. By the end of the course, the lady asked me to stay 30 minutes longer, gave me a huge tip and paid for a class in the future. I walked out of a twenty dollar class with one hundred and fifteen dollars, 30 minutes after I wrote that I would purchase the seventy-five dollar ticket for the young woman.

Yes, when we have unlimited money, we have the freedom to afford things we couldn't provide before. However, when we don't, we are resting in even better sovereignty; the freedom to watch God take care of us. The freedom to watch Him work!

Time and time again, I have watched God provide for me only the way he can. Years ago, when I was moving to the capital of the Bahamas for a new job. My parents and I traveled 3 or 4 times to meet with realtors in Nassau to find an apartment. After weeks of looking, we finally signed a lease on an apartment. However, hours later, after the ink dried, our lawyers said that the signatures were in the wrong place, so we had to re-sign the documents. During that time, a family friend messaged me to look at another condo. Since we realized the forms were no longer valid, we decided to check out this condominium first. Of course, the realtor wasn't too happy, but we saw this as a sign to be open to this new place. The condo we were about to purchase was a two-bedroom with one and a half bathroom, no washer or dryer. However, the condominium the family friend suggested was a two-bedroom, two and a half bathroom with a washer and dryer. SOLD!

We told them we were ready to sign, and they were excited. They hadn't put it on the market yet, and needed some time to talk with their lawyers. This time worked for us because I wasn't scheduled to make a move for a couple of weeks. However, the weeks passed, and the lawyers still weren't ready. The owners decided to be extremely accommodating. Knowing that I came for work, they offered to let me stay while they got their paperwork in order. For four months, I stayed free of charge in a gated community, in a very great neighborhood, with great amenities. By the fifth month, I began to feel a little guilty. I offered to pay the light bill and condominium fees, which totaled to $600. This payment would help them not to feel a financial pinch while they waited on their lawyers to get it together.

A year passed with my six hundred dollars a month "rent." My neighbors were paying their owners $1600-$2000 dollars in rent, while I paid only $600 a month, this could only BE GOD! After a year of trying to get their lawyers to deal with their situation understandably, they decided to put the apartment up for rent instead of sale, giving me first right of refusal to rent. God allowed this decision to coincide with the shut down of the job I had at the Hotel. I politely declined to rent at full price as this was not in my budget and moved in with an old high school friend, which was another blessing.

Every time I reflect on that year, I can't stop thanking God. Those 3-4 trips we made looking for a place, and there were so many places I wanted us to buy that just would not come through. God did not let one of those come through, because He wanted to do it. If He had told me on one of those trips that I would rent in an excellent neighborhood, gated community, pool, 2 bedrooms, 2 and a half bath with a washer and dryer for $600 a month for an entire year, I would have never believed, but that's what He did!

Learning to rely on God's provision and not just wealth, gives us the faith to know with or without money we will be fine. If we only focus on the accumulation of wealth and not on the one who brings the wealth, money has the potential to begin to control us. I once heard a story about a couple who had an enormous amount of money, so they called their financial advisor over to help them devise how to spend the money. How much to live off of it for the next 20 years, pay off all the bills, to take trips every year, to leave as an inheritance, and yet they still had money left over. So finally they decided to give this money to charity and just as the financial advisor was about to leave, they said, "but wait, what if we get sick?" The moral of this story is, no matter how much money you have, if your source isn't Christ, anxiety has the potential to creep into the way you handle your finances. How can money fulfill me if I'm often anxious about how to spend and what to spend?

Yes financial freedom to buy what I want, when I want sounds amazing. However I believe a better pursuit is to find freedom in Christ. He gives us the keys to open the doors, He makes the provisions for us. When we have the wealth, we don't have to wait on Him to open the doors. I do believe that God allows his children to experience both of these experiences, there are many wealthy Christians and many wealthy non believers. However I believe God wants us as His children to understand the freedom in Him first, so no matter how much money we have, we will still rely on His direction on how to spend. When our trust is in Him, we are no longer a slave to the wealth, because we recognize our real source.

Powerful positions equal influence and control

How many of us can think of a political leader or any leader whose character prevents them from having an influence on our lives? I believe we all can think of one, yet a lot of us crave powerful positions because we feel it will automatically help us to influence the masses. The truth is we don't need a powerful position to be influential, we just have to be willing to fight for a cause.

I remember the first time I heard about Meghan Markle and her courtship and engagement to Prince Harry. This 'ordinary' biracial woman, a divorcee with unwed parents, was about to hold a position in the Royal Family. Now some people may argue that her job lacks any high power or influence, but for me, that's debatable. She has the ear of some of the most influential people in the world, and that alone speaks volumes. However, what I want us to realize is that before she became a "Duchess," she already saw herself as worthy and influential. Not because she had an ok acting career, simply because with or without a title she knew her voice mattered, even from a young age.

At the tender age of eleven, she penned a letter to Proctor and Gamble* about a liquid dishwashing commercial. The commercial said, "Women all over the world are fighting grease stains." They changed it, at Megan's letter's request to "People all over the world are fighting grease stains every day". She was featured on Nickelodeon news at this time, for her courageous efforts to speak out against sexism. Therefore we don't have to hold a position of power to gain influence over others. Megan showed us that even an eleven year old who is courageous enough to speak up for something she is passionate about can influence the masses.

Another reason we like to be the person with all the power, is because we like to control the situation. As a writer, I'll admit I often have a hard time giving the pen of my life over to Christ. I've spent so much time writing scenes and endings in my mind, I often want to write my own story. However, if you've ever walked this journey with God, things don't always go as planned. No matter how hard we try,

God still has the final say. Deals will fall through, team members will disappoint you, and hard decisions are inevitable. **Proverbs 16:9 NIV** *"A man's heart plans his way, But the Lord directs his steps."*

Fame

I think a lot of people have a love/ hate relationship with wanting to be famous. On the one hand, most people want to be able to walk through a mall in peace, while holding on to their privacy. On the other hand, they want to be famous enough to feel seen and valued by others. The goal in life is not for people to see us, but for them to see Christ, that's in us.

Francis Chan* gave up his church because he heard his name called more than the name of the Holy Spirit. Most of us may not even recognize this, but I believe he knew how easy it is for us to get caught up in the attention and fame. He never wanted to forget who it was truly about, which is Christ.

I remember growing up feeling invisible and undervalued. I wasn't the popular one in the group. At sleepovers, when they had girls modeling in the contest, I was always told I had to be the judge or not be involved at all, because I wasn't pretty enough. For years I hid in the shadows of my popular friends. So the night I won my first beauty pageant, needless to say, I was on cloud nine. I went out, and people knew my name, without me ever having to introduce myself. I got in free at various events and always sat in the VIP section. I traveled for free. I met with dignitaries and received a brand new wardrobe.

However, months later, these moments of bliss were taken away when I competed in our national pageant and didn't even make the top 5. I was devastated, to the point that I sank into depression. God asked me one day, what changed from the day you won your local title? The answer was nothing. I was still a Queen, I may not have won the national crown, but I had a whole year left to serve the local title that had put me on cloud nine just months before.

Yes I was humiliated I didn't make the Top 5, but I still had a title: I was still a Queen. The sad thing is, as women, we do this every day. We forget who Christ said we are. We look to outside forces to see and value us when the recognition we receive from the outside world, like my pageant title, is fleeting. The longing to be recognized started from the rejection I received as a child and when I became older I thought a pageant title would validate me, but it didn't. As soon as I encountered another moment of rejection I no longer felt worthy and my worth regressed back toward my childhood insecurities.

Social media has engineered our minds to respond to followers and 'likes'. Unconsciously, we base our lives around it. We notice that pictures with a little more cleavage or butt action get more likes. Silently feeling moments of affirmation as people marvel at our photo, filling our tank of worth up, with their likes and comments. Whether you acknowledge it or not, you post a picture to get the attention of your followers. My response is not to stop posting. I also have social media, and I've also posted intending to get the attention of others. The thing is, what do we want to do with that attention? We have to be real about why we want fame ?

Although I do believe my entire pageantry journey was purposeful, it could never take the place of the first person who called me Queen; Christ. We must learn to pay attention to the moments in our lives when we didn't feel heard, seen, or valued. What first birthed the insecurity that gave us the hunger for fame. Who told us or made us feel as if we weren't good enough? Was it peer, a parent or guardian? Whomever it was, the enemy wanted us to believe in our minds that we aren't good enough, and that is simply not true.

Money can't save me like God can. I have watched God work miracles for my father's and brother's astronomical hospital bills. I put on my first ever production to a sold out crowd without spending a dime and no one knowing my name. My family members call me Kramer due to the number of blessings God has given me over and over, not because I'm more special than anyone else, but simply because I've learned to rely on the source, which is Christ, to guide me.

So although it's common to get caught up in chasing money, power, and fame. I try to remind myself daily of the many times Christ filled up my cup with His love and provision.

♥ CRACK THE CODE:

1. Write down a time when God came through for you when you had no idea where you would find the money?

2. What's the reason behind your social media posts? If you have a microphone for the world to hear, what would you say?

3. What does leadership mean to you?

♛ QUEEN HACKS:

> Learn to be a good steward over your money. Download the app *Spendee* to track your spending. Business owners- try *QuickBooks* or the online program *Wave* to track your income and expenditures.

> Use your social media to share a powerful message and then hashtag #theroyaltycode

CHAPTER 5

MINISTRY - THE GOOD, THE BAD AND THE UGLY

You did not choose me, but I chose you and appointed you so that you might go and bear fruit - fruit that will last - and so that whatever you ask in my name the Father will give you.

- Jonah 15:16 NIV

Usually, when people hear the word ministry, they only think of a pastor, deacon, elder, or some other clergy title. However, that's not the only form of Ministry that I want to address. I like the following definition the most "Ministry: is the spiritual work or service of a Christian or a group of Christians." The reason I like this definition is that it explains that as long as you are a follower of Christ, you can minister to someone else. We all have different strengths and interests, and if you are someone who likes to give baked goods and remind someone that God loves them when they're going through a rough time, then I believe that's a form of Ministry. So as we address the good, the bad, and the ugly moments within Ministry, I want you to approach it from that framework and not just the four walls in a church, religious or super-spiritual definition of Ministry.

Regardless if your ministry resides in the four walls of a church or if it's an unconventional approach to sharing Christ with others, its super important we allow God to consistently check our motives. It is so easy for us to get caught up in a "godly" thing that we are blind to the fact that we may be doing acts of ministry for the wrong reasons. Over the years Christ had to call me out on some of those reasons and I want to share them with you.

Good idea but not a God idea

As I mentioned when I moved back home from LA, I never intended for it to be a permanent move. I was coming home to recuperate some funds and head back, but God had other plans. So even though that year, I had some of the best moments I'd ever experienced in life, there were still some holes to fill. I was at one my lowest points financially, my love life was still non- existent and I was readjusting to a small island after living in two more prominent cities. I needed to regroup, so with the utmost of good intentions, I started a ministry, a small group for Christian women wanting to grow in their walk with God. I still to this day believe God wanted me to connect with every one of those ladies that were a part of this group, I think I just went about it in my way, instead of following God's way.

It was too exclusive, too vague to outside bodies, and lacked the covering of older and wiser counsel. The first few months were terrific; We bonded, laughed, talked about Jesus, and grew. However, slowly but surely, the enemy began to pick at our holes, and sooner or later, the group dissolved. I remain great friends with all of the women from this group, we honestly don't hold any bad blood, but the Ministry did not last. God revealed to me years later that it was an excellent idea to fellowship and grow with like-minded women. However, a good thing didn't make it a God thing.

He revealed that the reason my idea was a good idea and not a God idea was because it was self-serving. I started a group at a time when I wanted to connect with other women who loved God and who wanted to grow more in their relationship with him. Sounds pretty harmless right? So you can see why this would be a good thing. But that may have been a season, where God wanted to fill that void ALL by Himself and not have it filled by others. I thought because I was using a "godly" thing to fill a void that I was doing the right thing. However, God is not going to let anything or anyone get between the desire and void you have with Him, even if you slap "godly" on the front of it.

Wrong timing, I think getting together with other believers in a small group can be amazing, but we have to do it when God says to do it. Soon after, God told me grow where you are. I made up my mind, well then if you are forcing me to stay here, God, I need to create a circle of friends to be around, and I'm going to do it NOW! I purposely started it on a night I knew was going to be hard for me, because I wanted to be distracted and surrounded by other believers at this time. I could have just called some girls over to pray with me, but here I was ready to start a whole group before God's time, simply because I knew I was about to have a rough night.

Sometimes God is isolating us for a reason. However, if we take it upon ourselves to surround yourself with others in a season meant from pruning, shifting and developing, we can miss out on what God is trying to do. Because we have our own agenda of what our life should look like at this moment.

Isn't bringing others to Christ

When several groups of saved women get together, it helps to strengthen their faith? However, if we are not doing any form of outreach or making our circle open to others who also want to learn about Christ or grow in their relationship, how is that helping us to fulfill the mandate God placed on us? As Christians, we are mandated to go into the world and preach the gospel. So the concept wasn't biblically sound, because of the air of exclusivity. There is nothing wrong with having a safe place to grow, but we can't only be concerned about our growth while neglecting the growth and salvation of others.

I was blind and naive to Christ's concerns at the time and couldn't see why a group with such great intentions, just kept falling apart. The reason is that no matter what we do, it has to be led by God. These are just some of the reasons God called me out. When you evaluate your life, have you ever chosen a good thing over a God thing?

Seeking a Stage instead of Service.

We live in the age where female preachers and preaching couples have not only become popular and fashionable to Christian audiences, but they have begun to have a strong appeal to viewers without a strong faith background. While on the one hand, this makes them more relatable, it also sometimes places an ungodly desire within Christian women and men, to seek a stage instead of answering a call to Ministry.

We see the Facebook and Instagram photos and videos of large crowds, thousands of likes, red carpets, and in the name of making Jesus famous, we want the same thing. However, what we don't see is when these men and women go through personal spiritual attacks from the enemy. We don't know the intercession, the faith moves, the family challenges, and the tremendous responsibility that comes with shepherding a flock. With great "rewards" comes great responsibility.

This responsibility is why it's so important not to seek out a ministry but to remain still and steadfast and await a calling by our Father in heaven, and then let it be questioned and confirmed by a TRUSTED spiritual covering. We all may never grace a stage, and even if we do, we have to keep our heart positioned in a place of service because it can honestly become so easy for us to think we had something to do with the praise we may receive.

So why do we do it and a lot of times we ignorantly think we are going into something with the right motives, but somewhere along the line, it becomes more and more apparent that our reasons are selfish.

When we stop giving God credit for our gift

When we follow, watch, or read more of the persons we admire in Ministry more than we follow or READ the word of God.

You haven't started small, because you are waiting on God to open the door to BIG.

You are jealous and covet the lives of people who have a significant influence in Ministry the way you want to.

These are all key indicators you want someone to stroke your ego as someone prominent in Ministry instead of just asking God to use you right where you are. God has called some of us to one-on-one Ministry. May be you are the one who is going to have a one-on-one conversation with the person who will one day influence the masses. God is not going to use you, if you are seeking the glory for yourself, no matter how hard you try to make yourself believe you are doing it for the right reasons. God will be the one who examines your heart.

Whether we are pursuing a "godly" stage or a "secular" stage, the point is, trying to fill a void with a stage will never sustain us. People are fickle. One minute they are praising you, and the next minute they are judging your every move. So you have to remember not to let the praise get to your head and don't allow the critiques to get to your heart, because Church hurt is REAL. No amount of praise for doing "God's work" is going to fulfill you, validate you, or strengthen you when life's challenges come along the way. You will start to resent a stage because being at a certain level; a ministry requires you to pour into others continually. However, there is only so much pouring you can take. Your life won't sustain itself through your influence of the masses; you can only serve the masses from a filled cup, filled by Christ.

You are trying to position yourself to be "Found."

If I hear the term one more time that "Ruth was working in the field when Boaz found hern not twerking," I swear I'm going to pull my hair out. Now don't get me wrong, the statement is accurate, and I'm not saying that it's a bad thing to meet someone while you are involved in Ministry either. I hate this speech because that's the motive that a lot of women have when entering the Ministry.

They may be trying to gain brownie points with God or hoping to meet someone while they work along with them at the soup kitchen. No disrespect, but Christian women are some of the most thirsty women I have ever met. I know because I have been her, and I fight every day not to be her. Not the Christian part, because Jesus is the plug and always will be. However, I don't want to be a girl trying to follow the "biblical" principles in the hope of getting something from God. God is not a genie, nor is he Santa Claus.

Ministry is not a requirement or prerequisite for marriage, so I wish we would stop trying to serve as if it's a part of some checklist we have to complete before Christ deems us worthy for a mate, a baby, dream career, or vast amount of money. Serving in Ministry won't validate you for a man, nor for the masses that you may be trying to impress.

Serving in Church doesn't make you better than anyone else, so while I understand why Christian leaders tell women to get busy serving in the Church, I wish they would caution them at the same time that it's not a filler until you get what you want from God.

So as I mentioned before, there are no brownie points for being active in Ministry. This truth may be disappointing to some, but for me, it's refreshing. It's a reassurance that I don't have to earn a title with God. He doesn't call me worthy, chosen, or a Queen because I've served in 5 ministries, sat on the front row, and came to Church every Sunday. He thought I was worthy from the moment he created me. I can't earn his love, and I don't ever want to try because we all will fail miserably.

REASONS WHY WE SHOULDN'T USE MINISTRY TO FILL OUR VOIDS

The Salvation of others is in our Hands

No matter how much we tell people that God is their source, watching men and women of God hold fast to their faith is what brings a lot of people to Christ. It's like the saying goes, "you may be the only Jesus people ever see." This saying doesn't mean we are Jesus to them; It merely means the kindness and life we live helps others to grow in their walk with God. We hope it's not all their walk is about, but I believe it assists. Therefore we have a responsibility to shepherd them in the way of the Lord. So if our motives are not pure, we are putting their faith in danger, and we encourage someone to join our Ministry, we are taking on the responsibility to help lead them to Christ.

You see, the minute we throw in the towel after taking the mantle to shepherd lives, we are not only messing with our calling, we're messing with the calling of others. It sounds like a lot to handle, doesn't it, that's because it is. Ministry isn't glamour; it's telling God I'm ready for the weight that comes with navigating my faith walk and helping to carry others on the trail with me. We spend so much time trying to choose a ministry, when it's a calling. We don't just randomly choose a ministry, God usually gives us a tug in a certain area that leads us to a calling he wants us to fulfill.

I tried to run with all my might from ministering to single women. I thought to myself, if God is calling me to share a word with single women, then he is going to want me to stay in that season for my entire life, and "Aint nobody got time for that!" However, I had to get to a point where I realized that God had me struggle through this season because he needed me to be the vessel to help others through it. Whether he positioned me there for life or just a season, it's a calling he wouldn't allow me to ignore. Ministry has never been about you, but only about the lives that Christ has decided to touch through you!

It's been seven years since my first singles conference, and I honestly hoped I wouldn't still be in this season, but even when we don't understand why, God knows best. Sometimes it's the barren woman helping and encouraging other women who are praying for God to open up their womb, reminding them to hold faith. It's sometimes her watching their wombs open and trusting that God hasn't forgotten about her along the way.

The Enemy Will Come for You.

Whether you realize it or not, the enemy hates the fact that you believe in God. Therefore he is going to come after you ten times harder when you try to get others to believe as well. He's not playing with you, Sis! He doesn't care how cute your devotional video looks on Instagram, if you try to change lives, he will COME FOR YOU! Being in Ministry doesn't keep you from trials and tribulations; it puts the target for the enemy on your back.

I believe that it's more important to walk into our calling and not our yearning to please a fleshly desire for a stage or Instagram likes. When Saul was transformed into a believer and his name was changed to Paul, he quickly learned that he would suffer for the name of God. What kind of thing is that? How is that my introduction into Ministry - with the phrase "you will suffer for the name of Christ." Paul went after Ministry with such zeal and vigor, at all costs, ready to proclaim the name of the Lord. Most of us would have said, "Suffer, Nah fam, I'm good on that ministry thing!" That's because some of us enjoy comfort more than we are willing to be obedient. But the minute we choose happiness over obedience, the enemy will find a window to get in-between the call God has on our lives.

You see, some of us operate out of our emotions and not our obedience. Emotions will see two people at the conference and become discouraged. Obedience pulls those two people to the side and ministers into them, as if they were 2000. Emotions would want you to quit the minute someone drags your name through the mud or people call you a false prophet, obedience will have you clinging to the word of God for dear life as He guides you faithfully through that trying season. Emotions will cause you to reject God the minute He doesn't answer your prayer. Obedience will teach you to wipe your tears and remind you that God's ways are past finding out and that he is always working things out for your good, including your unanswered prayers.

When God calls us to something, our faith will go through tests. That's where our faith comes in. I used to believe faith meant just holding on to the promises of God and thinking that they will come to pass. However, one day, the Holy Spirit asked me to look deeper and realize that faith was more than just believing in the promises of God but having enduring confidence in the power, wisdom, and goodness of God. You see, when we say we have confidence in not only what God promised, but who He is, we won't get discouraged when the process to the promise looks different than we imagined.

We will see the five stones that David had to fight Goliath and have faith in God's power; We will see the five loaves and two fishes among the 5000 people left to be fed and have confidence in God's wisdom. We will see the ram in the thicket like Abraham did when he was about to sacrifice his son Issac and have faith in God's goodness. But, if we only set our eyes on the promise, the finished product, we give the enemy room to come in and plant seeds of doubt in what we have been called to do. When we study God's word, we realized he doesn't work that way.

If you are not with the enemy, then you are against him. So know that taking on a ministry for God is your declaration of war against the enemy. So when you step into the arena of that calling, make sure you're spiritually ready to fight!

Nations Are Waiting on your Obedience

Although some of us start or become involved in ministries that God hasn't called us to, I genuinely believe that there is a work for all of us to do to build up the kingdom of God. However, the more time we spend chasing the things that fill our emotions and ego, the more we are doing a disservice to those we have been carefully crafted by the creator to reach.

Karen Ambercombie is mostly known for the role she played as Ms. Clara in the famous Christian movie "War Room." However, what a lot of people don't know is that she spent years waiting on breakout roles as an actress. She entered the industry with the ranks of many famous black female celebrities, but either doors would close in her face, or she would have to turn down a role because it compromised who she was as a Christian. She always felt becoming a famous actress was a part of her calling, but for years no part served as her break out moment.

After years of disappointment, her husband's job moved them to North Carolina. Anyone with dreams of becoming a famous movie star knew that moving from Los Angeles to North Carolina is a guaranteed death to your career. So she began teaching acting and removed her focus from staring in a Hollywood movie and just began to steward over her portion. Then one day, right in North Carolina, a small production company came to town and auditioned several well-known actresses, but none was quite the right fit. You see, they had to review every actress acting history, and if anything fell in their resume that could compromise the message of the film, it ruined their chances.

So eventually they just reached out to local churches. One day Karen walked in there, and once she auditioned, they knew she was it. All the years of waiting, trusting, and wanting to work on how she would be able to touch lives with the gifts God had given her. Mrs. Clara was the role she was meant to play. If she had taken any of the previous roles she declined or was passed over for, she too would have been disqualified from filling this role. She was obedient in denying roles that convicted her spiritual walk, moving to North Carolina with her husband and actively passing her gift through the community to aspiring actresses. Acts of obedience that may have seemed random at the moment but were ultimately setting her up to be apart of a story that would be told throughout many nations.

Maybe you're like Karen and your time hasn't come yet, and God wants you to steward over what may seem small to you. Perhaps you were like me three years ago, and you're starting a group when God wants you to focus on Him this season. Whatever the call is, trust God to guide it. We must remember that when it comes to Ministry, we are nothing but vessels that God is eager to use for the kingdom, not vases that he is seeking to praise for its beauty.

♥ CRACK THE CODE:

1. Have your motives for Ministry always been pure, if not, what was at the root of the decision you made?

2. Do you feel God has called you to a particular form of Ministry, and you didn't answer the call?

♛ QUEEN HACKS:

> Everyone isn't always called to lead a ministry. Still, I do believe everyone can benefit from being in a community of like-minded believers, if you found that you don't have a community, reach out to your Church and find out if they have small groups or google "meet-ups" in your city! Pray about which community God is calling you to join.

> You feel God is calling you to serve but not sure where. Take this quiz and see which area lines up with your spiritual gifts. – https://gifts.churchgrowth.org/spiritual-gifts-survey/

CHAPTER 6

PUBLIC SUCCESS, PRIVATE FAILURES

"For there is nothing hidden that will not be disclosed, and nothing concealed that will not be known or brought out into the open."

-Luke 8:17 NIV

Society has trained us that "living our best life" or celebrating everything great about life involves a stunning makeover, traveling to a foreign country, mind-blowing sex, and a party in our honor. Without realizing it, some of us have centered our lives around significant milestones: Prom, Birthdays, Weddings, just waiting for these to happen, so that we can finally feel as if we're "living our best life." So what's wrong with wanting to celebrate our life in this way? Absolutely nothing, except at times we seek after these things with the wrong motives and desires and when we do that, we tend to move out of alignment of who God has called us to be.

Lipstick on a Pig

When I was younger, I developed a concept that light skin girls with curly hair were the most attractive girls. They were the ones that got all the attention, and therefore I believed anyone who didn't possess that skin complexion, or hair texture wasn't good enough. I ingrained this thought in my mind from as early as I can remember. Those were the girls that the older kids ran up to say, "isn't she so cute," the girls every little boy had a crush on, and the girls everyone wanted to be friends with. For a long time, I battled with marrying a white or light man to ensure that my child had a fighting chance of being one of the more revered bright skin girls. This insecurity isn't a truth I was proud of, but a fact nonetheless of how I viewed beauty.

As you reflect on your insecurities, I want you to think about what situations played a role in forming them. Because whether we believe it or not, all women struggle with them, including those light skin girls. My mom is light skin, and she told me peers would call her RED Hog. Children can honestly be so cruel, but the truth is none of us are exempt from society playing against our insecurities. We all fight personal battles of insecurity and fear of feeling unloved and unworthy. We think that we are too fat, too skinny, too dark, too bright or too pale. We struggle with skin textures, beauty marks, short hair, stringy hair, mysterious figures, crooked teeth.

However, no matter what it is that we deem beautiful or unfavorable about ourselves. Our father in heaven still sees us as beautiful. So if the media, your family, or anyone you have encountered along life's journey made you feel as if there was something about the appearance that made you unworthy, I want you to combat that thought and cast it out.

Ladies, please know you cannot combat these thoughts by straightening your hair, adding extensions, lightening or darkening your skin, liposuction, or by endless forms of makeup. If we don't change the way we feel about ourselves on the inside, we might as well be putting lipstick on a pig. You have first to recognize how beautiful you already are. There is nothing wrong with enhancing your natural beauty, but you have to realize you are beautiful before any enhancement touches your body or face.

Some of you might be reading this telling me that you have carried these insecurities around your whole life, how in the world do I expect you to jump up and decide to accept your differences. I want to remind you that because a darker skin black girl was brave enough to embrace her tone, the craze "My Melanin is Popping" was born. Because another black woman decided to embrace her natural curls, sales on perm straightening products plummeted as women of all ages and textures began to embrace their God-given curl pattern, myself included. Because a shapely woman didn't allow society to define her, the goal of being "slim thick" became a size more sought after then a precious size zero.

Society changed its standards of beauty repeatedly, so why do you allow conforming to the norm to dictate how you feel about yourself. In an ever-changing world, one thing we must remember is how we think about ourselves must take priority over everyone else.

As a former beauty pageant contestant and coach, I have made it a point to coach the girls I work with that a judgment against their physical beauty is hugely subjective. There is not one point system that can accurately judge what every individual in the world deems as beautiful, because beauty is truly in the eye of the beholder. So whether you walk away with a physical crown on not, know that you are a Queen before you even step on that stage. I'm not naive. I know some systems focus on nothing but the exterior, and that's good for them, but to me, an accurate pageant system raises your level of self-awareness, your confidence, your health and heart for humanity. Anything else that focuses on the exterior, as I said before, is nothing but lipstick on a pig. A beauty pageant or not! Sis, you're a beautiful Queen, so don't you forget it!

Party Like a Rockstar

I love a good celebration just as much as the next girl. However, as I have gotten older, I have realized that I don't need an "obligatory" get drunk, dance until your feet hurt kind of experience to deem this celebration as one for the books or one of the best nights ever. Movies and social media have drilled into our brains that this is how we make the most out of every moment, or else we're just not doing it right.

I remember heading to New York to bring in the BIG 30. This birthday was a milestone that had to be celebrated right, so we went sightseeing throughout the week and headed to dinner on the eve of my birthday. We were supposed to end the evening at some rooftop club, screaming at the top of our lungs, that I'm finally 30 once the clock strikes 12. We were going to bring it in true New York style. However, halfway through dinner, my friend looked at me with 2 hours to my birthday to go and said you're tired, aren't you? He was right, I was exhausted, I was happy to be 30, but this age also brought a new level of clarity. I don't care that everyone says I'm supposed to be living it up in some club to bring in this milestone. I'm exhausted, and I want to go home.

We sat on his balcony that had an epic view of the city, toasted with two glasses of wine, and at midnight, he looked at me and said Happy Birthday. There was no loud music, no DJ "shouting me out" from the mic or shots until I was dizzy in the head and couldn't remember what transpired. We shared a toast and the satisfaction that I had welcomed in a new era with a great friend.

It took a certain level of self-awareness for me to admit that that particular behavior wasn't me anymore. I was trying to fit in a specific box where the "best night of my life" involved an epic party. However, I didn't want to wake up with a hangover struggling to remember what happened the night before. Now I'm not saying you are never going to catch me doing my best version of the electric slide on the dance floor of a friend's wedding. However, what I am saying is partying in the club every weekend or feeling a mandatory obligation to party during a special occasion will no longer be an escape for me.

You see, the truth is, some of us party as a way to reward ourselves or to escape from the regular cycles of life. While there is nothing wrong with taking time to enjoy ourselves, partying is not the solution to fixing what we hate about our lives. It's a bandaid. The job we hate will still be there on Monday morning. Those unfulfilled dreams will again go unmet. You now just have less money to fund them. If you want to go dancing, dance because you enjoy it, not because of any reason, because a good dance is nothing but that, just a good dance. It's not a therapist, it's not a life coach, and it's not your savior.

We don't have to feel like old heads who have lost their zest for life because we prefer in-depth, intimate conversations and dinner dates instead of late nights at the club. If you got married young, don't worry, you haven't missed out on your golden party years no matter how much single women make you feel like you have. Take it from a girl who spent the majority of her 20's alone, and in the club, sore feet and random dudes asking you for your number or "just one dance" is highly overrated. A good party will never bring you the fulfillment you're searching for, so remember that the next time someone encourages you to ease your pain by hitting the dance floor.

Sexual Healing

When it comes to sex, some people view it as a form of expression, and as a woman, it gives them a sense of power to do it when and with whomever they feel. As a Christian, I have the opposite view. Surrendering my life to Christ means that I fully understand that while I have control of my body, I yield those desires to my father in heaven. I am not a virgin, so I'm not guessing when I say sex will not, no matter how good it feels, it will never heal me nor complete me. I do think it's a beautiful gift from God, but a gift designed for marriage.

The best analogy I heard about sex, compared sex to fire. When a fire is contained and controlled in a fireplace, it's beautiful; it brings warmth, it's safe, and it serves a great purpose. However, a fire outside of that contained and controlled space can be hazardous. It can destroy lives, homes, and other valuable things, I believe God wants us to realize this truth about sex. Sex was created to knit the bond even tighter between a husband and wife, not as a guilty pleasure to fulfill our selfish desires.

I remember the first time I tried celibacy; I had made it close to a year and a half. However, to win the heart of someone I wanted to be with, I decided to lay my celibacy vow down to prove how much I wanted this relationship. That was the worst sex I had ever had in my life. Not because the person was physically incapable of good sex; I had "great" sex with them in the past. However, sex is so much more than physical; It's spiritual and emotional. And emotionally, although our bodies connected, our hearts couldn't be further from each other. Instead of bringing us closer together, it was the final nail in the coffin that tore us apart.

Ladies, nothing we ever do will be good enough for a man who's not meant for us. I had to learn this the hard way. No matter how hard we try to fill the void we feel in relationships, sex won't fix anything. Nothing is empowering by giving that vulnerability of your body, soul, and mind to someone that hasn't proven that they understand the value of who you are. A wedding ring is a sign of their knowledge and commitment to how much they treasure you.

Queen, you're worth more than a one night stand, a promise of forever with the absence of a ring, or let's kick it and see. Tell him wedding bands will make you dance, signed papers will have you swinging from chandeliers, and a legal commitment will have you giving birth to his babies, but until then, he is just a few promises away from a potential broken heart.

I remember the rude awakening the Holy Spirit gave me right before I decided to take my vow of celibacy seriously. He said, Hear me when I say if you are sleeping with your boyfriend, his and your desires have already taken priority over God's will for your life. You have already decided that your fulfillment comes from a sexual relationship with this man and not from Christ. No matter how much you call on God, you are not living in His will. Having sex out of wedlock is not a modern-day version of Christianity, you are actively choosing to be disobedient to who God has called you to be. Ouch! However, this was a real talk! Now if this statement also convicts you, then yes, I have just decided to come to your house as well, to tell you some good news.

God is a God full of grace and forgiveness and second chances. His mercies are new every day. He took this woman who was extremely desperate for love and gave me a heart that desires to please Him more than I wanted to please myself. It's never too late for you to be real with Him about what makes this struggle hard for you; you just gotta be honest and let Him in.

So some of you may be saying, but Kerel, it's hard, and it is, so I get it. But the thing that I think that trips us up is that we've seen tons of women do it the opposite way and still end up married. So if you said this before, know that you are right, and that statement would be all well and good, if the marriage were the goal. However, I want you to ask a married friend if just being married automatically equals happiness or joy? I guarantee they will tell you that it doesn't and that there is a lot of work that goes into it, whether you wait or not. But not waiting brings a whole lot of insecurities with it. Will he remain faithful when you lose your sex drive during pregnancy or face a life-threatening disease? Maybe he will, perhaps he won't, but someone who has never had to practice self-control makes you question their ability to be able to do it.

If you couldn't surrender your sexuality to God before being married, what else won't you surrender once you get married? No matter what the media tells you, sex won't complete you. When the music fades, and reality hits, sex can't save a marriage, and it can't save you!

If you're married, don't give up on a good thing because the sex isn't what it used to be, spend your lifetime communicating and working towards making it the beautiful thing it was created to be. While someone else may have the wickedest slam, that slam won't sustain you years after you've destroyed the union that God has purposed for you. Us single chicks are out here are rooting for you!

Traveling to Escape Life

I remember one day in efforts to live out my single season to the best of my ability, I remember asking a large number of married women, one thing they regretted not doing as a single woman. Some of them had a laundry list that involved getting to know themselves better or education, and some said they honestly had no regrets. However, a recurring theme among most of the women was that they wished they had traveled more. Knowing that moving where and when I wanted was a perk of my single season, I made an active effort to try and visit a new city or country every year. And at first glance this seems like a pretty reasonable goal. How can broadening your horizons by seeing the world be anything but a good thing?

However, travel like other feel-good moments becomes a problem when we try to use our epic vacations as bandaids for our pain. When the answer to feeling incomplete, drained, or unfulfilled is planning a next epic vacation, we have unknowingly made seeing the world the antidote to our pain. Now sometimes a vacation is a part of God's journey to our healing, but He never intended for a fancy vacation to take the place of the eternal peace he has prepared for you. So yes, it makes our Instagram viewers gawk with envy at our exotic adventures, but is this trip a part of your purpose or a selfish positioning to make yourself feel better about other unfulfilled dreams in your life.

I remember one year making a trip to Germany, and although it was awesome having the chance to catch up with an old friend, the trip set me back a bit financially. And I was only adamant about going because I wanted to travel somewhere epic for my birthday, and I needed to fulfill my new country for the year quota. Truth is I didn't pray about if this was a trip God wanted me to take at this time, was I being a good steward over my money and would this experience be purposeful. Sometimes we escape certain traps. We tell ourselves I'm not sleeping with a random guy, I'm not getting drunk out of my mind or making money illegally, so I must be in alignment with what God has called me to do. Traveling is a healthy pastime that they encourage singles to engage in, so why can't I jump up and take advantage of trip opportunities?

Whether we deem an activity as morally correct or corrupt, anything that takes the space that Christ wants to fill, is nothing but an idol. That yearning and emptiness could never be quenched by "living our best

63

life," and although we sometimes do an excellent job of fooling the world that a passing moment of happiness is enough, it isn't.

He wants it All

In the last few chapters, we have unpacked a lot of things on "the checklist" that we, as humans, try to use as a source of happiness and fulfillment; Marriage, Dream Job/ Career, Children, Money, Fame, Power, Ministry, Beauty, Sex, and sometimes even Travel. And I'm sure for others there may be more. Still, if you have ever obtained at least one of these items at some point in your life, you would know that the yearning in your stomach for greater fulfillment still didn't magically go away. Some of your motives may have been different from mine, but the results remain the same, true happiness and fulfillment involves more than ticking an item on a checklist.

Christ designed us with a longing for fellowship with him. However, the enemy has convinced us that the longing resides in something other than Christ. **Matthew 6:33 NIV** *"But seek first the kingdom of God and His righteousness, and all these things shall be added to you"* isn't just a cute verse. Christ has to be the source, even when He gives you the vision, because when you remove your focus from Him, it only delays the vision.

When I think about focusing on God, I envision a ballerina twirling around and keeping her focus on an object so that she doesn't fall. The minute she loses focus of that object, she will fall. We are the same way, Christ is the object, and we are the ballerina. We start off trusting and focusing on God, and then we lose focus and begin to wonder what's taking God so long, and we fall. The wait gets longer than expected. Our desires get harder to silence, and eventually, we take life into our own hands and hope for the best!

Trust me, I get it! I'm not here to tell you choosing Christ's fulfillment over these things listed is easy, or that I have mastered every area stated here perfectly, shoot even Jesus asked God to take the cup away from him. I want you to know that as you cross each item off your checklist and you continue to search for that one thing that will make it all complete. Know that the crown from your real savior has been waiting on you all along.

💡 CRACK THE CODE:

1. What is your definition of living your best life, and why?

2. Which one of the goals did you relate to the most, and what do you feel your true motives are/were for wanting to achieve this goal?

👑 QUEEN HACKS

> Purposeful Traveling - Pray about where you will go. Then plan out your trips a year in advance and try to tie them to purposeful adventures: family time, career-focused conference, Missions. If you do feel led to explore a new city, find affordable ways to travel with websites like - Secret flying.com (affordable flights) or Mind Your house (house sit while you visit)

> Journal your journey with God - Letting go of idols can be challenging, but the best way to be content with your present state is to think of all the great things you are currently experiencing at this moment.

THE SWEET SPOT

If you don't like something, change it; if you
can't change it, change the way you think about it.

- Mary Engelbreit

The Merriam- Webster dictionary describes the sweet spot as the area around the center of mass of a bat, a racket, or the head of a club that is the most effective part with which to hit a ball.* I grew up watching my brother and sister play tennis. During this time they were always encouraged by their coach to try to hit the ball at the sweet spot so that they could achieve the most effective swing. That's what I want to encourage you to do, approach life in the most effective way, we're often missing the ball, because we are focusing on the wrong thing. Focusing on a "checklist" as a means to fulfillment can become daunting, especially since we can't always control the outcome or timing of our desires. Therefore I want us to hit the sweet spot by changing the way we think about these desires. So exactly how do we do that?

The First step: acknowledge It's not about you! When we accept Christ as Lord and ruler of our life. His plans become our plans, His desires become our desires and His timing becomes our timing. **John 16:33 NIV** *"I have told you these things, so that in me you may have peace. In this world, you will have trouble. But take heart! I have overcome the world."* During the pain that often comes during seasons of waiting, we trust that He is working it out for our good. He has already told us in life, we will have pain, but through the pain, He is still in control.

When we acknowledge this verse, we are no longer surprised when troubles come. We simply learn how to cling tighter to the source. We have to choose to no longer lament over why isn't God doing it but place our focus on God's purpose for this season, asking Him what He wants us to learn? How and where He wants us to serve? And how He wants us to experience joy?

The Second step: Gratitude! One way you can start experiencing joy is by starting each day, writing at least three things you are thankful for; trust me, it's harder to be depressed when we take the time every single day to give thanks. Change your focus from everything you lack, to daily recognizing everything you have. Joyce Meyer once said, "It's so easy to forget how blessed we are! That's why maintaining an attitude of gratitude is something we need to do on purpose."

The third and final step: develop a growth mindset. Take all the energy you have invested in focusing on a checklist you can't control and invite God to direct your areas of growth. The second half of the book provides a detailed framework on how you can intentionally grow in three critical areas of your life; spiritually, personally, and professionally. I want to encourage you to change your focus from seeking happiness from an achieved item to learning how to enjoy the journey of growth.

It takes a whole lot of practice for any tennis player to hit the sweet spot on the racket every time. So don't beat yourself up if you don't become the Serena Williams of personal development overnight. I'm not asking you to become instantly perfect at hitting the sweet spot; I'm merely asking you to try.

SPIRITUAL
DEVELOPMENT

CHAPTER 7

HOW DOES GOD SEE YOU?

*So you are no longer a slave, but God's child and since
you are his child, God has made you also an heir*

- Galatians 4:7

Now I am not naive enough to believe that everyone reading this book has a super-connected relationship with God, and some of you reading may not have a relationship with Him at all. So I get it, looking at life through the lens of how God sees us isn't going to be something we all naturally do. So I want you to first think about how do you see you?

I want you to take a minute and ask yourself the question, "Who are you?", like legit, close your eyes and ask yourself the question. Go!

Did you do it?

Ok, chances are the majority of you may have not even thought of an answer. It's honestly one of the most complex questions to ask someone because we rarely think about this question. If you were able to come up with an answer, you might have described yourself by your profession. I'm a doctor, a lawyer, and event planner or maybe you described it by a role of high importance to you, I'm a wife, I'm a mother, I'm a mentor. You also may have described it by your character or personality; I'm passionate, I'm observant, I am an intelligent woman, or maybe you define yourself by your accomplishments. No matter which category you went with, we tend to often describe ourselves by associating our response with the most important thing to us. If it's our career, that's the first thing that comes to mind; if it's family, then that's the first thing.

However, how many of us, the first response to this question is I am a child of God?

Because when you become a child of God that becomes the foundation of your identity, none of your other titles matter if you don't understand what it truly means to be a child of the King.

The world usually has the power to lead us down a spiral that has us chasing wedding rings, babies, dream homes, and careers. We are seeking identity and reassurance in these things because it seems like everyone tells us, when we do this, we will be accepted, admired, loved, and revered.

Only when the world knows my name then will I feel fulfilled, then I would have finished what I came to do. However, God says before you took your first breath, you were all those things to me.

Queen, in case you didn't know, God says

You are chosen - 1 Peter 2:9

You are loved - John 3: 16

You are blessed - James 1:17

You are redeemed - Ephesians 1: 7

You are forgiven - 1 John 1: 9

You are seen - Jeremiah 1:5

You are wanted - 1 John 3: 1

You are accepted - 1 Corinthians 12: 27

You are a fighter - Psalms 18: 39

You are royalty - 1 Kings 9:5

You are a Queen - Isaiah 62: 3

The foundation of your existence, the joy you have been seeking, has always been available to you. You don't have to compete or prove your worth to anyone.

However, this truth begins to make us question, if I have everything I've ever needed in Christ, are we saying that goals and dreams don't matter? The answer is no! God wants us to pursue the things He has called us to pursue. He also wants us to do it through the doors He has opened and for a lot of us, that is the hard part. The minute we receive a revelation of the gifts and talents that God wants us to use in the earth, we sprint ahead of His promptings and try to make it happen all on our own.

We sometimes say, "God gave me a heart for entrepreneurship. I know He wants me to open my own business." Yes, but does He want you to spend the first ten years on a 9-5 learning the dos and don'ts of operating that business? "God gifted me in acting, I just know he wants me to move to LA and pursue this dream." Maybe but maybe he wants you to teach drama to high school kids for the next 15 years and will blow your mind with an international film without you ever having to leave your hometown. Goals and dreams don't go against God's plans He has for you, but he has to be able to trust you with His plans. He has to know that you won't worship a specific position or relationship more than you will worship him. He has to know when the fame comes you are going to step out of the light and point the attention to Him. He wants to ensure that you know that you're merely a vessel He wanted to use during this season.

God wants to know that He is first, and everything else that makes up your identity is second. If the titles below never grace your biography, is God enough?

If you never become a -
Wife
Mother
Grandmother
CEO
Aunty
Minister
Grammy Award-Winning Singer
New York Times Bestseller

World thought Leader

Doctor, Lawyer or Insert Profession/Title Here

Entrepreneur

World Traveler

President/ Prime Minister

Do these titles mean more to your identity than being a child of the King? Can you honestly say, if I never hold any of the above titles, I will be content, fulfilled, and reassured of your best because your plans are better than anything I could ever dream?

If I'm honest, this was a hard statement for me to make — especially title number one. For years I waited, dreamed of, and craved the opportunity to hear someone call me their wife. Like legally not the play, play boyfriends throwing around the word wifey without a smidge of commitment. The title wife, I wanted that to be a part of my identity. So why was this word so powerful to me, why did I need it to be the way the world defined me. Whether we admit it or not, some of us believe that a wedding ring tells society that you're not a "left-over." You're wanted and chosen. You have the honor of someone wanting to stand before God and everyone he loves to declare that you are the only woman in his life. That was a pretty big deal for me!

So how exactly did God walk me through the fact that this title could never be worth more than the title he already gave me?

First of all, when I became a child of the King, my life was now designed to please an audience of one, so whether society deemed me worthy or not, it didn't matter.

Secondly, I've had suitors who wanted to make this commitment, but I chose God's will over a pursuit that wasn't quite the right fit at the time.

Thirdly, if God needed me to be married in this season to fulfill the purpose He placed on my life, I would be married, end of the story. My sole mission on earth is to bring others to Christ. Therefore if God needed me to do this through my marriage at this time, I believe He would have already ordained me to be married. So although I may want a marriage in this season, if I don't have it yet, God is saying I don't need it right now. God makes no mistakes. As long as I remain faithful and obedient, He will continue to lead me down his best path for me. I have to be able to trust that.

So what do we do, when trusting who God says we are, gets harder than we hoped? What do we do when we've learned the foundation, but everyday living is merely easier said than done?

Fall in love with God

When you love someone, you not only get to know them, you learn to trust them. The people we love, we talk to them every day, they're the ones we run to whenever we want to bounce new ideas off of someone or need advice. God wants to be this for you, and for me. The more He becomes the friend that we can be open and honest with, the more we will begin to trust Him.

Have you ever had a trait about you that you felt was so innate to who you are as a person, but it doesn't coincide with the word of God? Like it's tough to fight because this particular trait or feeling has always come naturally to you. However, just because something usually comes natural to you, it doesn't mean it's your identity. We can't change the word of God to fit what's convenient for us. It could be a generational curse, and environmental influence, or a reflection of someone we admire. Still, I guarantee you if it goes against the will of God, it's not a part of the identity God created you to be. God doesn't make mistakes, so again we have to love him enough to trust this truth.

Romans 6:6 NIV *"For we know that our old self was crucified with Him so that the body ruled by sin might be done away with, that we should no longer be slaves to sin".*

Every one of us is born into sin, and every day we fight our sinful nature. However, accepting Christ means that we refuse to be ruled by our flesh, and we submit to the spirit of God. That's who we are.

I remember my first year of college, we would wear the shortest skirts, halter tops, and the highest heels standing out in the cold winters

73

of Canada waiting to get into the club. We threw back shots of alcohol, waiting all night for the one guy we had a crush on to dance with us, ready to shut the club down every weekend. That was me. If you asked me back then, who are you? I'm a girl who likes to have fun, and that fun involves dressing half-naked and partying with my friends on the weekend. Ok, maybe I wouldn't have verbalized that out loud, but mostly that's who I was.

When I got serious about my relationship with God, those things no longer phased me. I remember recently being convinced to go to the club to celebrate my best friend becoming a doctor. I had a stoned cold look on my face the whole night. This club thing was no longer my scene, this wasn't me. I had changed, and one of my friends said it to me, "you've changed, you got boring," and you know what I said-

"You are right, I did change, and I am so over this. Can we please leave now."

I trust who God says I am. Even when it goes against what my friends had once known me to be. When it goes against the culture and when it's the least popular decision to make. Every day I am on a journey to be more like Christ, that's who I am.

John 14:15 NIV - *"If you love me, keep my commands".*

Study your gifting and Talents

We build on our identity by studying our unique gifts and talents. Growing up, were you someone making masterpiece art on your parents' wall? Were you the organized one, who had to make sure that everything was in place? Were you the one with the lemonade stand trying to sell 2 dollar lemonade? Or were you the one never afraid of confrontation and always willing to get up in someone's face to prove a point? These are signs of things that come naturally to you, and even the negative traits are hints to God wanting you to dig deeper to allow Him to use this trait.

Don't be afraid to allow God to be creative. Kirk Franklin was a terrific songwriter, he had charisma, and at 17 had someone ready to pay him to put his songs on an album. There was just one problem. He couldn't SING!!!! Most of us would have said, how can I be a songwriter, create a singing group, put out albums, and get paid for this for the rest of my life if I can't even sing. If we are still enough to hear God's creativity in who He is shaping us to be, we can recognize how He wants us to affect lives.

You don't have to be in ministry to be operating in your God-given gifts and talents. If God called you to be a massage therapist, maybe clients notice how you give them an inspirational card at the end of every session. They may begin to wonder what makes you so thoughtful, positive, and generous (cards cost money). That's your opening that it's nothing but the God in me. Instead of spending your life chasing all the things that you believe will make you happy, watch how much fulfillment comes from allowing God to show you who He created you be.

Spiritual Food

We've all heard the old saying, "What goes in, is what comes out". If you eat healthily, you will feel healthy, and you will see great results. We become what we continually feed ourselves. Do you know how many people started drinking wine with popcorn after becoming a Scandal fan? They loved what Olivia Pope represented with her posh outfits and quick lingo. They wanted to have this identity so bad fans even ate like her, a TV character. Individual schools create an environment that dictates the behavior of the majority of students who went there. Students adapt to this way of life; it became a part of their identity.

That's how our relationship with Christ is. The way you talk, dress, eat or communicate, everything you do is a reflection of what you have exposed yourself to and therefore begin to believe about who you are as a person.So if you want to know who God says you are, read His word, surround yourself with people who have a similar style and interests as you. For example, spiritually, I follow Pastor Michael Todd, Pricilla Shier, Sarah Jakes Roberts, and Joyce Meyers, to name a few, and while I don't try to mimic who they are, a lot of what they say and do, influences who I am.

The point is, you are what you eat. I remember that I never cursed in high school. Yet, after my first year of college, I was cursing like a sailor. I couldn't figure out what happened until I realized I had been hanging around people where cursing was second nature and not a big deal to them. We learn so much of our behavior from our environment, we must pay attention to what we feed ourselves.

Kingdom Identity

Our Kingdom identity is so important when seeking to fill that void we feel when we are on a quest to achieve the many goals in our life. It's a reminder that we are no longer in control. If we controlled the outcomes of our life, then we would be justified in being disappointed when we didn't get the job, lost the bid on the home, or suffered several miscarriages. While we are human and will experience the pain from these circumstances, we can rest knowing our creator never makes mistakes. As **Romans 8:28 NIV** says, *"ALL things work together for good for those who love and trust God"*.

Having a relationship with God gives us the advantage of the race ahead. In the movie *Overcomer*, at the last minute the runners were allowed to wear earbuds in one ear. The main character's father coached her through her ear bud. As a former cross country runner, he knew the exact route and speed she should take every step of the way. In previous races, she had never even made it to the top 10, but on this particular day, she won. I believe the difference was, she had someone whom she loved, and trusted, someone she knew had experience to guide and encourage her along the way. He told her when to slow down, when to pick up the pace and when to make calm, and collective strides along the way. She wasn't in front of the race the whole time. In fact, she didn't run into first place until the VERY end, but she trusted when he said to keep a steady stride, and by the end of the race his coaching led to her victory.

The question is, who is in your ear? If the wrong person is feeding you information they may tell you to speed up to everyone who is in front of you, to keep up with the others because your current face value makes you look like a loser. You're not a loser because you're 40 and not married. You're not less of a woman because you've been married for five years and haven't gotten pregnant yet. Being a stay-at-home mom, does not make you lack purpose. Our journeys are all different, but every one of them is purposeful!

No matter what it looks like right now, there is victory at the end. God cares about your dreams and goals, but if you don't know who He created you to be, you could be chasing a goal or dream that doesn't even line up with the good and perfect will He has designed for you.

♥ CRACK THE CODE:

1. Think about the first time you fell in love romantically, what things did you do to show your significant other how you felt? Have you ever done any of these things to get to know God?

2. What do you feed your soul? What music do you listen to, the books you read, things you watch, or accounts you follow? What are you putting into your spirit daily?

♛ QUEEN HACKS

> Download the Bible app; they have wonderful Daily devotionals of relatable everyday topics to keep you learning at your pace and help you learn more about real situations you are currently going through.

> Digging Deeper - Download the *First Five* app. It has daily devotionals. But more so, it focuses on studying scripture passages in the Bible and breaks down the passages for you to get a deeper understanding of God's word.

CHAPTER 8

DISCERNING THE VOICE OF GOD

My sheep listen to my voice; I know them, and they follow me.

- John 10: 27

So you've decided to surrender everything you thought would bring you joy, and you give your life over to God, now will all your goals and dreams come to pass? Not necessarily. Now I know what you may be thinking, Kerel, you went and read my whole file, told me to see myself the way God sees me, and now you're telling me there isn't some easy fix. Yes, this is what I'm saying. Learning how to trust God and keeping him as your foundation will take a lot more work.

What I had to learn as I matured as a Christian it's not that God doesn't give us what we want, He gives us the desires He places in us, which eventually become what we want. I remember before I wrote my first book, I never dreamed about writing a book. At a certain point in my life I hardly even read books, why would I want to write one. God changed my heart to want what He wanted, my desires became His, and I began to fall in love with the process.

So how do we know? How do we know when a desire is us hearing the voice of God or just us eagerly coveting a selfish ambition? The truth is we don't always know for sure. I would be lying if I said that as Christians we always get it right. We're human, we make mistakes and sometimes we do hear wrong or hear in part. A lot of times, our confirmation is found in hindsight. Yet, there are ways for us to gain a higher and more precise understanding. Because the truth is, the more you know God, the more clearly you will be able to hear Him.

I love the example Pricilla Shirer gives on hearing the voice of God. She tells the story of how non-family members could call their house and mistake her brother's voice for her dad's voice, but not her. She knows the distinct difference between their voices because she has spent so much time with both of them that she knows their voice. Once we accept Christ, we have the privilege and honor to hear the voice of God.

So how do we get to know God? We spend time with Him. We read His word and learn His character. I'm always seeking God's word to see how I should make the decisions that will guide my life. For example, in dating, there are three scriptures I usually use as a basis to decide if the person I am interested in, is worth entertaining. **Matthew 6:33 NIV** *"But seek first the kingdom of God and His righteousness, and all these things shall be added to you."* If I don't get a sense that God is first in your life not only verbally or on your Instagram profile, but in your actions and way of life, that's the first red flag that this is probably not the right person for me.

The second verse is **Proverbs 18:22 NIV** *"He who finds a wife finds a good thing, And obtains favor from the Lord."* I believe men were created to chase, and therefore if I feel no form of pursuit in his actions towards me, I'm not interested. If I'm making all the calls, I'm suggesting all of the dates, and I'm the one bringing up next level conversations, chances are this isn't a person interested in pursuing me. It doesn't mean we cannot be friends, he just isn't it. His lack of pursuit tells me where to gauge my emotions because scripture tells me, if he saw me as His wife, he would be in search.

Finally, the scripture **Amos 3:3 NIV**, *"Can two walk together unless they are agreed?"* If he has recognized God as first in his life and is actively pursuing me, yet I cannot see how God is aligning our purposes together, this is also a red flag. We may get along great but may be heading down two separate roads for the kingdom.

I don't feel these scriptures are some magic formula in finding the man God has for you; these are just scriptures I feel God has highlighted for me when guiding me through the dating process. I genuinely believe God cares about every detail of our lives, and if we study the Bible, we will begin to gain a greater appreciation for His character and His will for our lives.

Surround yourself with wise counsel

This can be spiritual mentors, accountability partners, or men and women of God that you have never met, but have begun to follow their ministry from a distance. I remember opening night for my very last play we were performing in Nassau, and my lead actress, who had no understudy her flight was 6 hours late! All-day, we wrestled with canceling opening night. Around midday, my brother and I decided if her final connecting flight didn't leave by 5 pm, we would cancel the show. The show was scheduled to open at 8 pm. If she didn't go by 5 pm, it would be too late to warn audiences not to come to the show. Around 4:45 pm, she and her plane still hadn't left, and I remember feeling a sense of peace and said to myself, we're going to have to cancel the show. Trying to reassure myself that it's going to be ok, it will all work out, and I remember telling my plight to this lady sitting in the audience.

I didn't know this lady from a can of paint, but I told her God already gave me peace about this, the show won't go up tonight, and I'm now ok with it.

She said, "You never know she still may make it time."

"Nah, we said we would give it until 5 pm, it's 4:45 pm, and they haven't left yet. There is no way she will make it time"

She said, "Don't give up, its not 5 pm; I know you think you heard the show won't go up, but wait, you may have heard God wrong."

I wanted to tell her my communication with the Father is just fine, but I remained quiet and listened, 4:55 pm we got the text that they were boarding the flight. We made the call the show was a go. With flight arrival, customs, and change of wardrobe, our curtain opened up 45 minutes late. I had never started a play that late in my life. However, that was the best performance our cast had ever given. It was also the best audience we had ever had. They laughed at every joke, clapped during every performance, and greeted us with a standing ovation at the end of the show. That night was one of the best experiences of that entire performance. I had heard wrong but was humble enough to trust the wise counsel and wait and watch God show up in a significant way.

Confirmation

Finally, God speaks to us through confirmation. However, we must be careful about it because our endorsements still have to align with the word of God. I remember being in New York and for five blocks the name of my ex was engraved in the concrete ground that I was walking on. This totally freaked me out, but it was also my "sign" that we were meant to be together. Right? No WRONG! These "signs" were nothing but the devil playing with my emotions because at the time God wasn't first in his life, he sure as heck wasn't pursuing me at the time, and our lives were not in agreement. So while God does use signs, we must be careful that it's Him and not the enemy or us.

I remember at one point in my life, I was praying about where I would live during my last few months living in the city I was in. I had three months before I was about to make a big move, and I needed a temporary spot. So while praying, God dropped a girl I went to high school with into my spirit. I knew she had a two-bedroom because I had randomly ended up at her house earlier in the year. But still, we weren't that close of friends. We even had a season in life where we would be more defined as enemies. Although we had moved on from that previous debacle, roommates might have been a bit much. However, I couldn't shake the name. I felt like God was saying I want you to ask her to live with her for three months. Minutes after, this same woman "coincidently" messages me a selfie of her and my mom. They were currently at the same conference, while I was battling whether or not to send her a message. I was floored! Right then I took the prompting of the Holy Spirit and asked her to pray about me living with her for three months. She came back a few days later and agreed she felt a peace about it. Friends were nervous about if this dynamic would work, but it did! We nurtured our friendship, gave each other their space, and encouraged and prayed with each other about our future goals and dreams. Of course, I irritated her with my loud devotional morning talks with God, but in the end, I feel this season was a great source of growth for both of us.

So maybe you've had moments where God came in and co-signed something He was already building in your heart. Don't ignore it as random or coincidence. Try the spirit, seek His face because more than anything, God wants to build a rapport with us. He wants us to be accountable. The Bible says faith without works is dead. We have to be willing to do our part. A lot of times, we have goals and dreams, and something happens that gives us a glimpse that it may come to the pass, but we don't want to do the work to make it happen. Even when God aligns us with his plans for us, there is still work that we have to do. My roommate's situation would have never worked if I never intended to pay her rent, decided to eat all of her food, or expected her to take care of my every need. God opened the door, but I still had to do the work.

Discerning the voice of God is not only about learning the avenues that God uses to speak to us, but it also understands that sometimes God tells us "Yes", "Not yet" and "No".

There have been moments in my life where I have watched my goals and desires perfectly align with God's will for my life. From winning my first pageant to international speaking engagements, travel opportunities, and more. I have watched God open the door to endless blessings in my life. There is honestly so much to be grateful for. I want to remind you that He is the same God who is willing to do that for you, too. We tend to feel if we let go of the grip of the things we want and become obedient to live how God wants us to, we will never be able to enjoy the things that make us happy. We focus so much on the rules of religion and forget that Jesus didn't die for you to concentrate on religion; he died because he wants to build the best relationship with you.

He wants to laugh with you, make you smile, and comfort you. He wants to bring you a sense of peace, joy, and serenity that will have others looking at you with admiration. Secretly saying to themselves there is just something different about her. There is an unexplained confidence, she doesn't "have it all" by the world's standards, but her glow tells a different story. Her smile says that without it, she alone is enough. When you say 'yes' to God, He gladly opens up the doors to the 'yes' He has designed for you.

Prayer

I genuinely believe that when we pray, God tells us no, not yet or yes. I recently experienced the hardest no I ever received from God, when my brother passed away at the end of this summer. Everything in me thought that this would be nothing but a recovery process. I knew it wouldn't be easy, but I never dreamed that when I moved my brother out of his apartment and started doing physical therapy with him, that this would be his last few months I would ever get to spend with him on earth. We went through three daily affirmations. He would repeat -

1. I am healed
2. I will fully recover.
3. God has a bright future for me.

I even wanted to create a hashtag as we documented the recovery process. I suggested #kennyproadtorecovery. He thought it was just ok and suggested #ineverlostmypraise. I thought to myself, quite lame but hey since it's about Jesus, then fine. Every day I would pray to God to help him to regain his ability to walk, to speak clearly, and to get back on his feet.

But week after week he wasn't getting better, he was getting worse. He had to go into the hospital as his strokes kept recurring. They found blood clots all over his brain. He took the blood thinners to decrease the clots, but nothing worked. My brother was slipping away right in front of me, and I couldn't believe it. I knew God could do the impossible; I knew the testimony he would be able to give would be so great. God had to save him. I consistently received affirmations and confirmations from friends and families of people they knew pulled through impossible circumstances. God was going to do it. Right?

As the weeks went on, I started to have anxiety. We were always told to come to the hospital for meetings where they told us to prepare for the worst. That this was it and that we should start to say our goodbyes. I couldn't understand why we had to fight so hard. We went on a fast, always prayed, surely God was going to work a miracle. Then the day came when they asked us if we wanted to take the breathing tube out of him. He had become too ill to be airlifted. We were reaching the end of the finish line.

I made one more call to a contact in Cuba, and had them read my brother's file, I needed to know if there was a strand of hope anywhere, I wanted to see it through. They reviewed his file and told me there was nothing they could do to help him regain mobility or stop the progress of his condition. Whether we found out months before or days leading into it, these were my brother's last weeks on earth. At 37 years old, with so much to offer the world, God visited me that evening when reading that email and granted me a peace that passeth all understanding. Despite the weeks of fighting, fasting, and praying, he was about to be called to a better place.

This thought was crippling, but God reminded me that this earth is just the place we pass through, and our eternity is with Him. He gave my brother a precious gift of months of a renewed fellowship and relationship with Him. At the beginning of Kenton's treatment, we began to do bible studies together, and eventually, my brother independently did them on his own.

84

I thought God would save Kenton on earth so that others may come to Christ because of what he did in Kenton's life. God said; "*You let me worry about how I will bring the masses to me. I healed Kenton when I took him out of his pain. I recovered all the years he lost when he rekindled his relationship with Me and is now enjoying a bright future in heaven.*" And through it all, Kenton was right; he never lost his praise.

I thought a win for the kingdom meant saving his life on earth. God said a victory for the kingdom is when I got the opportunity to save his soul. His eternity is with me, and there is no higher win than that. God's ways have and will always be past finding out. Was He capable of saving my brother, of course, He was, but this wasn't his design for my brother. Kenton had completed his assignment on earth, and as hard as it was to see it, this was God's good and perfect will.

God knows a 'no' can be heartbreaking, but they are also filled with so much wisdom if we are willing to open ourselves up to trust Him. My brother died two days after I received this revelation. And while my relationship with God gives me strength and peace to get through this season. There are still random bursts of tears, overwhelming moments of sadness as I reflect on our precious memories, and indescribable pain when I think about all of the beautiful moments we will never get to make. Yet still, I trust Him.

Sometimes God says yes, sometimes he says no, and sometimes he says not yet.

God's timing is so perfect. I remember wanting to leave a job so badly, and no matter how much I applied and searched the newspapers for postings, nothing was happening. Years later, God brought my dream job to fruition, and I was super excited, a kid in a candy store for about a year. However, I wasn't on this dream job for more than a year before God transitioned me into becoming an entrepreneur.

This 'no security' lifestyle was never for me, but again a perfect example of God turning his desires to our desires. I had no security, but I was waking up every day doing the kind of work I loved to do. God knew I would enjoy a life where I could do the work that I loved to do. However, the unpredictability, dependency, and patience that comes with the way God wanted me to do it, as an entrepreneur, He knew I needed time to mature and blossom into this woman, a role I'm still learning and navigating every day.

God tells us not yet because he sees the big picture ahead. He knows what we can handle and what we can't. Christ knows you will enjoy the honeymoon phase of marriage, but because you are still at the beginning stage of building your brand, you will begin to resent the everyday duties of a wife as they start to set in. God knows you would love the feeling of becoming a world-renowned success but will begin to feel guilty if he opened up that level of fame, at the cost of neglecting your young children during this season. Hindsight is 20/20, but I guarantee you if God is making you wait, it's because he is saying the current thing you have a "not yet" on is not what you currently need. God didn't take the day off; he didn't miss your call when you asked Him to open that opportunity to go off to school. Trust that you may be in a season of not yet.

The first step in the right direction of releasing our idols is recognizing the difference between God's desires for us and our selfish motives. The truth is, this is hard because, honestly, a lot of us want things that are positive, morally sound, and at times sacrificial. Surely if it's a good thing, God would want us to have these good things too. But, I learned a long time ago, just because it's a good thing, it doesn't mean it's your good thing, and if it is, His timing for it will always be better than our own. So we must learn to turn the volume down on our desires and do the work to turn the volume up on His.

💡 CRACK THE CODE:

1. Do you remember a time you heard God's direction or felt God speak through someone to you and watched the confirmation take place in your life? What was this experience like for you?

2. Have you ever thought you experienced God, and you heard wrong? What was that experience like for you?

3. Is there something you feel God has promised, and you are waiting for it to manifest? What confirmation do you have that this is a word from Him?

♔ QUEEN HACKS:

> Develop a prayer wall or board in your room, and when you have something in your heart or a word you feel God has spoken to you about, write it on your prayer wall and watch certain dreams come to pass. (I did this with my winning a Bahamian Icon Award, now it happened three years later than I expected, but I watched God manifest it, it's refreshing to watch his words come to life)

> Watch the Bible project on Youtube. It's animated versions of books of the Bible. When you're first getting into reading the word, connecting the stories tend to be hard to understand. Seeing them unfold and explained through animation makes it clearer.

> The Bible series on Netflix is also an excellent introduction to understanding the character of God.

> Attend a local Bible study to gain a stronger understanding of God's word.

PERSONAL DEVELOPMENT

CHAPTER 9

TRAUMAS AND TRIGGERS

The Lord is close to the brokenhearted and
saves those who are crushed in spirit

- Psalm 34:18 NIV

Whether we care to acknowledge it or not, I believe we all have our "issues." We all, at one time or another, went through a painful experience that has played a role in shaping us into who we are today. We can't change the past, but I think a big part of developing ourselves personally involves us facing those traumas and triggers. We must be aware of how they sometimes hold us back and how, at times, they can also fuel our greatness.

Oprah Winfrey often tells the story of watching her grandmother hang clothes outside and her grandmother telling her to watch because this was what she was going to have to do to make money one day, and she remembers thinking to herself, no, she won't. Even though she went through a dramatic experience of being sexually abused, having a child at a young age, and then having a child die, she still made up in her mind that these traumatic experiences wouldn't result in her hanging out clothes for work. She allowed her pain to make her stronger. It became her fuel. I believe we all can turn our pain into purpose. But if we are unwilling to admit that that pain is there and what triggers it to appear, we will always be fighting a losing battle.

Childhood Scars

There are some things we remember about our childhood, some we block out and some parts of it we don't remember at all. When I was younger, I remember my brother had a friend that came by on a motorcycle. I begged my brother to allow me to go for a ride; he said no, but after a few minutes, he went inside to answer the phone, and I tried to go for a ride quickly. Before I could sit on the bike correctly, my leg accidentally touched the muffler burning a significant amount of skin off of my leg. A scar that is still there to this day, while this didn't cause any emotional wounds, sometimes we encounter experiences that do. And it creates an invisible scar that continues to stay with us.

Every time I look back at my leg, I remember the incident. It's like the physical pain felt in that moment has been embedded in my brain. However, there are so many experiences I don't remember at all. The other day a family friend showed us a childhood video of us at their baptism, I am telling you that experience felt so brand new it's like it never happened. That's how life is, some things we remember, and others we don't, but even the memories that aren't at the forefront of our brain still play a role in how we function today.

Unfortunately, a lot of women reading these words went through physical abuse, sexual abuse, parental rejection, peer rejection, family drama, and some even chronic diseases. These scars are not just another thread in your story; it's a part of who you are. As hard as it is, we have to be willing to identify how the incident made us feel in the moment, how it makes us feel now, and how it controls how we interact. Our curiosity for sexuality, our self-worth, life choices, and so much more, are all fabrics woven together from things we experienced as children. One of the most beautiful gifts that you can give yourself is to embrace the highest level of self-awareness.

Daddy issues are a real thing, whether your dad was not emotionally present or not physically present at all. That sense of belonging doesn't just go away. You must recognize how it made you feel and remind yourself of the one who you've belonged to first. Even after you do this, it will be a journey to reclaiming the woman God called you to be. Make no mistake; God will use everything you went through to shape you. Some of the fear we feel when facing our struggles, will cause you to begin to question God, asking why didn't he protect you? How could Christ allow this to happen to you? It's not fair that everyone else didn't have to go through it, how could he let such an innocent child endure the kind of pain that you experienced?

Queen, He sees your scars, and I guarantee you He never left your side. You were born in a world of sin, and He knew that this sinful and imperfect world would challenge you, that's why He made the most significant sacrifice by sending His son to die for you. I don't know why it happened to you; however, I do know **Romans 8: 28 NIV** *"And we know that in all things God works for the good of those who love him, who have been called according to his purpose."* I know that it's fuel to make you more compassionate, resilient, wise, and sensitive to the pain in the world, that only you are crafted to tackle because of your experiences. Your obedience and faithfulness to a father you may often question, I assure you are not in vain.

Loss of a loved one

I believe losing someone you love changes your whole outlook on life. At first, you're extremely heartbroken, a little jaded, and consistently filled with despair. But as I mentioned in a previous chapter, you can choose to feel this kind of pain, or you can open up your arms to the father and experience healing, restoration and joy.

An article I read that helped me during my journey of grief reflected on **Philippians 1: 21-24 NIV Paul** stated-

"For to me, to live is Christ and to die is gain. 22. If I am to go on living in the body, this will mean fruitful labor for me. Yet what shall I choose? I do not know! 23. I am torn between the two: I desire to depart and be with Christ, which is better by far; 24. but it is more necessary for you that I remain in the body."

Did you read that verse, this dude is saying that he is torn between living and dying. I'm sorry. How? This verse utterly confused me until I

91

learned that Paul realized something that was hard for us to understand - to be with Christ is far better than to be here on earth. This verse set me free. We spend so much time trying to store up our treasures on earth, so much time trying to live our best life on earth, that death feels like the end. However, when we have accepted Christ, it's the beginning!

Death allows you to realize that the material things, the goals you keep trying to tick off, can't go with you. The only thing that is worth anything after death is your relationship with Christ. Therefore I cry because I miss the memories, but death no longer leaves me jaded and filled with pain of regret because I know the one who holds my future.

I had so many plans for my brother and it's natural that sadness continues to greet us because of the memories we made. However, the Bible tells us in **Proverbs 16:9 NIV** *"In their hearts humans plan their course, but the Lord establishes their steps."* Today if you are struggling with the pain of a loved one you've lost, as a child of God, know that they're living their best life with Christ.

Victim or Victor

In life, we can't always control what happens to us, but we can control how we decide to respond to it. Whether its a traumatic situation or death of a loved one, we live in a fallen world. So how do we deal with the inevitable pain that we often encounter? You have to decide that I'm either going to be a victim or a victor.

A victim points the finger at the other person. If my dad were there with us, I wouldn't have had self-esteem issues. If my mother knew how to love me correctly, I would be much further in life. If that person didn't betray my trust; if this person didn't break my heart and the list goes on. I'm not saying the pain you went through was fair, nor was it right, but living a life of pointing the finger at the person that hurt you is continually giving them control over you. You can't change what they did, nor can you change them, the only thing that's in your power is to change your response to it.

It's easier to accept that it's someone else's fault for the way we behave. We make excuses for negative behavior, claiming that I've always been this way; This is just who I am. Is it? Is it who someone told you who you were, or is it a part of the hard shell you created to cope with the pain of a traumatic experience. You chose to be selfish, cynical, unforgiving, prideful, and secluded. You refuse to do the work that came with allowing a situation to make you better and not bitter.

Triggers

As humans we are often subject to triggers, triggers usually ignite something you didn't realize was buried inside of you. Sometimes it's the things that people do to set you off, but you never explored why. If a particular smell, location, or words send anxiety up your spine or causes an instant panic - pay attention to it, it may be something you have buried and need to deal with. I'll share an intimate trigger with you. I have a big freak-out session when a guy tries to touch my face. It's because I have the insecurity that my chin isn't always as smooth as a baby's bottom. I went through laser surgery years ago but it didn't work. So regular trips to the spa for waxing is always on the agenda. I'm seriously contemplating laser again, but until then, this insecurity has me straight trippin. Most of the time, I don't even explain the freak-out session. The guy is usually just sitting there like a deer in headlights, wondering why I almost gave him a karate chop.

I'm fully aware of this trigger, and until now, I have NEVER publicly talked about it. Instead of facing this insecurity and admitting that this is just a part of my genetic make-up, I often play the role of a victim and try to ignore it and hope that everyone else will too. The minute someone is bringing attention to it, I get feisty about how they shouldn't just randomly touch someone's face, when I haven't dealt with the insecurities going on internally with me.

We all have a choice whether we want to become a victim or victor when we face life's challenges. A victor is willing to do the work. That's not only remembering the identity that Christ gave you, but it also includes being brave enough to speak up when you need help!

Get a Therapist

In the black community, therapy is a negative thing. Just take your problems to Jesus. Ah yes, Jesus is a miracle worker, but Jesus never said that there was something wrong with Jesus and some therapy. We can't ignore the pain we feel from incidents that build fear and rejection. Maslow's hierarchy of needs shows that after our basic needs of shelter, food and water, we need a sense of belongingness and love. If we experience anything that creates a barrier to this kind of love, the results can be life-altering, and there is nothing wrong with allowing someone to help you to explore this pain.

What's the point? The point is, you will understand why certain things make you angry or agitated. Your level of self-awareness will abundantly increase. You know how hard it is to communicate with a friend or someone you love when you can't fully articulate precisely why you have trust issues, why you shut people out, or why you're incredibly horrible with money or time management? You can't grow or change certain negative habits if you don't know where they have stemmed from in the first place. Do you think you are a hoarder by accident? You're not. It's more profound. You emotionally eat for a reason, and your anxiety has a root. All of the things that stopped previous relationships, caused barriers between you and your children and have you leaving every job you ever go on, may have something to do with you. You have failed to introduce yourself to the real problem. These are the things you bring to therapy.

You are not weak for admitting you need help. You are weak when you know that something isn't right, but you refuse to do something about it. Talking about it may seem futile, but it's usually not until we say something out loud that we can face it. I spent eight years as a counselor in the school system. Therefore, my colleagues in the field became my therapist. I remember one day sitting with my colleague, and she asked me, "Why do you even want to get married?" No one had ever asked me this question; I didn't even have the answer at the moment. It was just something I thought everyone wanted. However, what it revealed about my motives and selfish desires was mind-blowing. I talk a lot more about this journey in my first book, *The One Year Challenge*. However, I want you to know, winning looks like being vulnerable, open, and honest with someone who can talk you through your struggles, desires, and wants.

Transform your Mindset

We spend so much time trying to control the outside world around us. However, actual progress only occurs when we learn to control our minds.

In August of last year, God woke me up and said, I'm tired of the devil stealing all the things I have planned for you, and you should be too! GET UP!! You are under attack, and it's time for you to FIGHT.

I was utterly confused, what battle, what attack, I'm living Jesus, I'm okay, right? NO, you are not, you are existing and WAITING! Waiting for something to fall out of the sky and save you. It's time for you to get out of this slavery mentality, stop wandering around this mountain, and LEVEL UP! Let me tell you something friend, if you feel you are in a wilderness season, it's not because you are waiting on God, TRUST me you're not, He's waiting for you. God made me disconnect from social media, cut out ALL distractions, get on my knees, and give Him the keys; He was getting ready to SHIFT MY MIND!

When focusing on the restructuring of my mind for my finances, God used a financial blog by Natalie Bacon* to transform my mindset. She shared this simple yet powerful visual.

Thoughts -- > Feelings --> Actions --> Results —> Repeat

As a man thinketh, so is he. If I think I'm broke, I'll feel broke. Therefore my actions will reflect someone with a broken mindset, and the results will be BROKE Kerel. However, if I think that I'm in transition to wealth, I'll feel better about creating that wealth. I'll take action by asking myself questions that force me to figure out how to create even more wealth, then how to manage and track my current wealth. The results, well, I'm not asking you, I'm telling you, it's innovative ideas that I put the work into to create MORE WEALTH!

- The first week, I found over a grand of my money in my house from a project my team completed months before.

- I was offered and went on TWO international speaking engagements, a four-year-old dream, offered and manifested in less than 60 days!!!

- I recovered my six-week recording of a small group study guide shot back in 2016 that I thought I lost on a damaged hard drive.

In some instances just being open changed a lot of my results; with the speaking engagements it was a matter of vocalizing to the right people things I wanted to do, and those things eventually happened and with the drive, I didn't give up on it. I didn't call it a loss. I took it to the people who could potentially fix it and asked them to try everything possible to get it fixed. A lot of us don't realize that a lot of the work we need, starts with the way we think about our lives.

The final step is one of the most important, and that step instructs you to repeat the process! You will read this book and feel empowered. So why does it leave, why does a self-help book, build you up and then you return to business as usual. You stop the gratitude journal, you go back to being insecure and low self-esteem spirals, but why?

You have to be willing to continually work on the way you think, feel and act to see the results in your life transform. A book, a motivational speech or really good talk is nothing but a spark. You have to do the work of constantly repeating the shifts in your mindset to see the actual change in your life.

Accountability Partners and Mentors

The third and final step in doing the work involves the people around you. If you are a new Christian and none of your friends are about that Jesus life, I guarantee you it will be pretty hard for you not to slip back into your old lifestyle or grow in this new one. If therapy is the best thing for you and the people you around make mental health sounds like a figment of your imagination and not a real thing that a lot of men and women face every day, you will never get the help you need.

My mentor was one of the first people who told me to stop referring to myself as broke. I have been an entrepreneur for the last three years, and anyone who has financially traveled this role without a 9-5 to accompany it knows it can be challenging. I use to refer to myself as broke A LOT; I don't know how many times a day, until one day she stopped me and said to stop using that word. I said, "Do you want me to be delusional and lie, cause if you look at my bank account, you will see, I am not lying, I'm broke!" She then told me to start adopting the phrase that "I am in transition to wealth."

Let's dig a little deeper, why didn't I view entrepreneurship as a transition to wealth phase instead of a broke period. We are told to go to college to get a good stable 9-5 job and then retire when your 60. This venture that God had me on when he told me to be an entrepreneur was scary. And I didn't deal with my thoughts and negative feelings about it, feelings that my culture taught me about not following the 9-5 guidelines. Our surrounding is what puts limits on us. There are people around you, including family, who are subconsciously putting you in a jar with a lid on it. You can't do the work, surrounded by limiting beliefs.

The creator of Spanx, Sarah Blakely said her father rewarded them for failure growing up. He would ask them every day, "What did you fail at today?" At first, this question confused them, but eventually, this trained their mind to continue to try. He conditioned their mind to realize failure isn't a bad thing. So even though it was hard trying to get her business off the ground. She didn't sit in rejection, fear, and insecurities. She rose above it. She faced it head-on because her surroundings fostered thinking of resilience, hope, and faith. A healthy mind will lead to a healthy heart and a healthy life. If you want to develop personally, you have to look every negativity you have directly experienced in the eye and DO THE WORK!!!!

♀ CRACK THE CODE:

1. Is there a traumatic or painful experience from your past, that you believe played a role in shaping you? If so, do you think it made you better or bitter, and why?

2. What are some limiting beliefs that you tell yourself about yourself and your ability?

👑 QUEEN HACKS:

> Download the app www.regain.us- for virtual therapy experience

> Make your Lock screen of your phone or your screen background and encouraging scripture or motivational quote. My current local screen says: Seek the Kingdom of God above all else. Matthew 6:33. We look at our phone always, let the screen remind you of what you can overcome.

CHAPTER 10

WORK ON YOU, FOR YOU!

You can receive all the compliments in
the world but that won't do a thing

- Unknown

As women, we sometimes find ourselves in two different scenarios: Either we are overwhelmed trying to be everything for everyone else or frustrated because we are working on certain things about ourselves in hopes of achieving a goal we have. We spend a lot of time hoping that God will reward us with a particular outcome because of all the work we have done. No matter which avenue we choose, none of these paths involve us wanting to work on me, for me.

The truth is sometimes our actions aren't Christ led. Even those of us who claim to be Christians, our daily activities tend to seem to rarely involve Christ's direction, because external forces usually motivate the work we do. It's so easy for the outside world to determine our self-worth. These forces are the reason for us pushing so hard, and this is a scary place to be.

We want to be the best wife, best mom, best daughter, best friend, best employee, best boss, best committee member for everyone else in the room, except ourselves. However, when our self-worth is hanging in the balance of receiving this title, recognition, or acknowledgment from someone other than Christ, we open up ourselves to be an open target. We set ourselves up to be on the receiving end of potentially feeling unappreciated, betrayed, or overlooked. We live in a fallen world, and therefore our actions cannot be tied to external praise or recognition from others, because eventually, they will fail us. We have to live for an audience of one.

So what does this look like? What does it look like when we begin to develop and fashion ourselves for Christ. Sometimes it makes perfect sense, and other times, it's confusing to everyone else. Yet, I think the right place to start is taking a page out of Simon Sinek's book, and *Start with Why*, evaluating our life and asking ourselves, why am I doing this?

In Simon's TED Talk*, he talks about the Wright brothers who were unknown, had no money, and no connections but knew that if they got it right, transportation by air could change the very world we live in and how we can connect with others, and it did. However, the person we don't often hear about is Samuel Pierpont Langley. At the time he had the fame, the money, the resources and yet still couldn't figure out how to create the very first airplane. All the odds were in his favor, but he was doing it for the wrong reasons and, therefore, never quite figured it out. Once the Wright brothers had a successful flight, he gave up on his quest instead of working with them to make this invention better. Samuel's why wasn't strong enough.

What we choose to develop & how we choose to build it usually comes down to the reason why we want to pursue it in the first place. How many times do we ask ourselves this question? The psychology background in me can't help but to always ask why. I imagine that at times some of my friends may get very angry with me during conversations because I'm continually asking the question, but WHY? Why would you do that? Why do you feel that way? If the root doesn't lead back to prompting or leading from God, then I urge you to challenge your involvement or to the very least, your level of participation in that particular task or venture.

Every one of us has a purpose for our lives. There are things that God created you to do that only you can do. So the more time we spend developing and focusing on areas that cater to our agenda and less to Christ's agenda, the more unfulfilled we will feel. If you are still struggling with if the direction you are going is Christ-led, versus you-led, I'll encourage you to read the chapter a few pages back, that talks about discerning the voice of God. Take those lessons along with what I believe is also very important to God, balance. Begin to feed your mind, body, and soul with the things that propel you toward that God-given purpose and not derail you.

Fuel for your mind

I remember talking to a friend the other day, who was a little upset about feeling like she wasn't in a mutually beneficial relationship. She thought that she invested more in their friendship than the other person. When I asked her why she couldn't distance herself. She said I don't know; I need to learn how to give up on people sooner. I said that's the problem you have right there. The way you look at things. You're trying to force a relationship with someone who isn't as invested in building one with you. Distancing yourself is not giving up on them; it's setting boundaries that protect your peace and sanity. I don't care how close you are or even if the person is family, toxicity is toxicity.

After we spoke, I started to wonder why did we see the solution to the same problem in two different ways. Why was my friend looking at distancing herself from someone as a negative thing? Her wording made it sound like she was doing something mean "giving up on someone." We want to be courteous to everyone else but ourselves. However, it's mean to allow yourself to continue to be treated as second rate by someone you hold in such high regard. So why do we sometimes see the world this way? Well, what you put in is what you get out. Mental food is just like the spiritual food we talked about in Chapter 7. I believe if what you watch, read, scroll through, or surround yourself with doesn't uplift you, empower you, and reassure you of your value, you won't be able to see your worth.

The way you choose to remind yourself of your value consistently is up to you. It can be placing inspirational quotes around your home, reading transformational books, listening to podcasts, watching motivational videos, learning a new skill, or one of my personal favorites, purchasing everyday products with an inspirational message. I have tried all of these practices and they always feed my mind and increase the way I value myself. Take a moment and reflect on this past week and evaluate what intentional decision did you make to feed your mind?

Fuel for your Body

The year was 2007 and it was the first time my body went through a complete transformation. I lost over 50 pounds, got regular back and face facials, monitored my eating habits, had an impeccable skincare regimen, and enrolled myself in grooming classes. I was getting ready for my first beauty pageant. However, once my pageant season was over, the weight slowly came back on, the regimens eventually went out the window, and the monitoring stopped. I spent about five years preparing and competing in a total of 7 local and international pageants. Some I won, some I lost, and others I placed, but it wasn't until years later that I realized that it was more about the journey than the destination.

When we focus on having great skin, great hair, and a slim waist for a particular milestone or on impressing someone else, the minute that end game goes out the window, so does your regimen. It's not always "happy" weight after you get married, sometimes that's just the results of your routine kicking back in now that you have already achieved the goal of looking your best in your wedding gown. We all do it - we set an external goal in mind. The problem is we can't control external things; the only thing we can change is ourselves. So the commitment has to be self-motivated.

The hard reality about self-motivation is a lot of us don't have it! We have to be honest with ourselves and learn to staff our weaknesses.

Remember the list we made of things we are fantastic at and things we don't like. Pull that list out and staff the weaknesses. Can't wake up to go to the gym- get a trainer, can't afford a trainer- get a gym buddy; you can help to keep each other on your toes. Prepare meals on the weekend, or if you can provide it, invest in weekly healthy meals delivered. Make hair and skin appointments in advance, so you keep it! Single women- use "boring" no date Friday and Saturday nights to go through the skin and hair regimens you have been saving on Pinterest. Married women- hire a nanny, if not full time, once a week so that you can get some ME time in. Can't afford one-reach out to a single friend or wife with no kids and ask if they mind sitting once a week. They may even do it for free! You have to find time for you! Money helps if you have it, but if you don't, be creative. You owe it to yourself and your health.

If you want things to change, you have to be proactive. Sitting down saying I wish I were skinnier, my skin was smoother and that my hair would grow and flow more, won't work. You can't want these things into existence; you have to plan, take action, and TRACK your progress when working on you!

More Fuel for your Soul

I can always tell when I've missed a long period of devotion time. I'm stressed, overwhelmed, and so much more likely to step into something I shouldn't be doing. I don't know if you have ever felt that way. Like you would usually shake your head at that bad driver, but today you want to run him off the road and curse him out? No, just me? Ok! The point is those days are when I'm depleted from my me time with God. He gives me peace when the world seems chaotic. He restores my soul.

So what do I do during my time with God? Sometimes it's just a walk on the beach to clear my head. A prompting to go in the community and give back, and sometimes it's worship music in the car. Because of the rough season I went through recently, a friend made me a mixtape, well a mix CD, I should say. It made me feel really nostalgic but also helped a whole lot. Those songs fill my soul and give me strength on the harder days. I'm also not a neat freak, I'm the opposite, but I'm learning to be more organized. Doing less multitasking and more focusing is also helping me to feel more centered with Christ and at ease.

At the end of the day, feeding your soul is the most important out of the three. Because if you didn't get it by now, that is the entire premise of this book. Your personal, spiritual, professional development, everything you do, to live a more happy and fulfilling life rests on the foundation of Christ.

I once heard the quote:

" Girl read your Bible,
You can eat all the kale,
Buy all the things,
Lift all the weights,
Take all the trips, trash all that doesn't spark joy,
Wash your face and hustle like mad,
But if you don't rest
Your soul in Jesus
You'll never find
Peace and purpose. "

So yes when working on you remember to feed your mind and your body, but more importantly remember to feed your soul.

Do you love you?

You have to make falling in love with you a priority. I remember during a season where I was struggling with singleness, I found an inspirational message on youtube where the interviewer talked about the fact that when we are dating, we love to ask the question, "Do you love me?" When the better question is, do you love you? Some guys get irritated at girls with low self-esteem and sometimes can't seem to understand why. The inspirational message explained that it's because if you don't love you, it will be hard to fully love anyone else.

When you are working on you for you, loving you and putting yourself first no longer becomes an afterthought. It becomes a requirement. It doesn't matter what the end game looks like because we have learned to be in love with ourselves.

Loving you is finding balance in the choices you make and what you allow into your life. Loving you also means knowing when to say no. Sometimes you have to say no to things that don't align with your values, and sometimes they do align, however, saying yes at that moment takes away from the other things that are more important to you.

Sometimes loving you looks like reading an hour every day when you want to hang out with friends. Sometimes it looks like being open to your mom wanting to interrupt you while you're doing work to have a conversation with you. Balance (This is low-key hard for me! I hate when people interrupt my flow, but Jesus is still working on me!)

Sometimes loving you looks like a strict diet, a plate of 50% veggies and five days a week workouts.

And sometimes loving you means accepting the dessert because you deserve to treat yourself every once in a while - balance

Sometimes loving you involves putting yourself on a budget so that you can manage your funds properly.

And sometimes loving you consists of spending some extra funds on a day at the spa or an occasional retail therapy treat - balance

The keyword here is balance. Weekly spa trips, endless desserts, and daily Sephora shopping are not a treat. That's complete self-indulgence, and your pockets or tummy won't thank you later.

One of my mantras in life has always been growth is everything. However, growth is extremely uncomfortable, and in a world that craves comfort, we rarely want to do the work that forces us to be the best versions of ourselves. When you think of persons who hold royalty positions today, their lives are filled with structure, discipline, and boundaries. All set in place because it comes with the role, they're not even allowed to have social media for goodness sake! But with everything they have to trade in, some perks come with the role, that I'm sure we all at one point or another would love to enjoy. For me, it's the travel opportunities, for you it maybe something else. The point is, it all involves an excellent level of balance. The ratio of discipline vs. fun won't always seem equal, but I believe it will lead to a sense of fulfillment.

So to the family woman who puts everyone's needs ahead of her own- stop trying to be everything for everyone else except you. I know I have never been in your shoes. But I also know that I have heard enough wise wives and mothers say that you cannot pour from an empty cup. I remember in the first few weeks of becoming a caregiver for my brother, I forced myself to the gym, for my sanity. My days were becoming overwhelmed with physical therapy, eating schedules, doctor visits. Some days devotion, and workouts were the only things I did for me. However, I had to find something to hold on to, while still fulfilling a role that was super important to me, being there for my family. The thing is, if you're not your best, you can never give them your best. Queen, work on you for you!

To the single woman who is active in a million ministries, got your job duties and responsibilities on lock, and you are beating that face every time you step on the scene. Yet, still, you have seen no promotions, lack genuine fulfillment from these filler activities, and wonder why your "Boaz" has yet to notice you. Sis work on you for you.

We can do all these things and may never get a thank you. We can try our hardest and that Boaz or "goal" may never come. Therefore our joy cannot be attached to things out of our control. Joy is in the journey and not the destination. If God has granted it to come to past, I guarantee you, He does not need your help, it will come to past. So while we can't control the results, we do have the power to make the choices to develop the areas that God is leading us through.

God calls you a Queen, Chosen, bought for a price, but you do you call yourself Queen. You have to show people who you are. If you're not calling yourself or treating yourself like a Queen, no one else will. If we wait for others to define us, instead of setting it for ourselves, we will often face disappointment. I believe when we do this, the people, opportunities, and rewards that are meant to find us will. When you walk with God, your glow attracts what's for you and repels what has been sent to distract you. Work on you, for you!

🔦 CRACK THE CODE

1. Write down 5 Things you value but put five spaces under each value. Then under each value, write three activities that coincide with each listed value.

> For E.g.
> Value - Faith

1. Read the Bible in the morning

2. Watch at least one sermon through the week

3. Listen to only worship music in the morning

👑 QUEEN HACKS

> Put your water in a motivational bottle that will inspire you to drink it more.

> Download Pinterest or start being active on Pinterest again. I became active on Pinterest again when I realized that it was a social media app that helped me focus more on personal growth. Whatsapp, Instagram, and Facebook keep me in a comparison or consumer mode when Pinterest is less focus on the social aspect of what other people in my circle are doing. It continues to feed me the things that I search for, that help me grow.

PROFESSIONAL DEVELOPMENT

CHAPTER 11

FIND YOUR TRIBE
& LOVE THEM HARD

I've learned that people will forget what you said, people will forget what you did, but people will never forget how you made them feel.

- Maya Angelou

Our final focus for the areas of growth that will help to transform our lives is professional development. The reason I felt led to include professional development is because we spend most of our lives contributing to our life's work. Think about it, most of us spend 8-9 hours of our day on our job or engrossed in our life's work. However when pursuing our careers, a lot of us leave God out until we are praying for that promotion, landing that new client, or getting a raise. The problem is, a lot of us aren't even really positive that the path we're on is the path that Christ has called us to pursue.

Previous generations would pick a profession and stay there for life. Regardless if it aligned with where they felt God was leading them, they stayed because it was comfortable and familiar. However, what if it was where God told them to be. Some of us *(i.e., me, I'm some of us, some of us is me)* judge them because they never left, but to them, they are sitting at jobs and holding positions their parents could only ever dream of, and if that's God's will, this perfectly ok. Our generation wants to do the same. We too want to level up and challenge the status quo, and nothing is wrong with that as long as God is leading the ship. The thing is, if we are honest, He isn't always leading.

I think an essential thing for us to also remember **Isaiah 55:8 NIV** *"For my thoughts are not your thoughts, neither are your ways my ways,"declares the Lord,"* God is sometimes sending you in the opposite direction. We have to be able to trust that, especially with our life's work. So in these final chapters, I hope to shed some light on how he has helped me not only pursue my God ordained purpose but also find my tribe and love them hard!

Start with Why

Starting with why isn't only a key to personal development, I also believe it's also the first step in letting God direct you in professional development. As Christians, we often pursue a specific area, because God called us to that area, but I want us to go deeper. Why do you feel he called you to that area? Why is God saying your most meaningful work will be at the law firm, in this studio, or on that non- profit?

A good indicator of our why usually rest in the problem we enjoy solving for others or the thing we enjoy doing that brings value or joy to others. Ever since discovering Simon's book on *Start with Why*, I realized that my brand management company is a small firm that believes that "Growth is everything." We provide small business consultation and training and development because we love to watch people grow. We love to see the light bulb go off, the dots connect, and the ah-ha moments when someone's vision for their life's work becomes a little clearer, and that's why we do what we do. God has fueled me with the desire to help others grow.

Now you may argue that many people discover their true passion without having a relationship with God. And I would say that you are right. I have watched self-actualized people pursue their passion and find comfort in meaningful work. However, the difference in the way someone who has allowed God to lead, is that as Christians, we do it all for the kingdom. We also know that His will is more important than

110

the monetary attachment to our work. We may think of a million different ideas and ventures that may lead to more wealth than some of our current projects, but when God is first, we don't pursue it unless we have the clearance from Him. I know that He has shown me over the years that ventures He has led me on are worth far more than the money I would have gained from my ideas and pursuits.

So what's your professional why? Is it rooted in Christ? Does it align with exactly who He created you to be? If not, then why are you doing it?

Team Builder, Entrepreneur or Both

After we discover our why I feel it's also important for us to realize exactly where God is calling us to serve.

Before we dive into whether your pursuit should be as an entrepreneur, team builder, or both, take a look at the list below and pick which one sounds most like you. Be honest and see which one fits your personality the best!

Team A

1. Responsible
2. You embrace Failure
3. Willing to sacrifice personal desires for the greater good
4. You're a Risk Taker
5. Generally Optimistic
6. Great Communicator
7. Self-aware
8. Great at conflict resolution
9. Innovative
10. Adapt well to change

Team B

1. Loyal
2. Reliable
3. Humble

4. Great at collaboration
5. Flexible
6. Likes a certain level of consistency, safety & comfort
7. Goes above and beyond the call of duty
8. Responsible
9. Realistic
10. You fear failure

If you chose A as the tier that most reflects who you are, then you just may be called to entrepreneurship, you're a visionary. You love the responsibility of starting small and growing while you lead a team to a designated destination.

If you chose B, you are a hardworking Team Builder; you love building something bigger than you while also impacting the people around you along the way.

If you can't choose between the two, then maybe you are cut out to do both. This decision requires you to trust God to walk you through the different seasons that these opportunities will bring.

If none of these sounds like you, then maybe the trophy wife or soccer mom is more your speed! Funny enough, I've met women who have said that trophy wife or soccer mom is their dream career, so if that's you, more power to you, self-awareness is an essential tool in life! Still, I want to caution that even if this is our desired destination, let's make sure it's God's will for our life.

TEAM BUILDERS

How to Find your tribe

Once you have done the work, you know who you are in Christ, you know what's personally important to you, and you know you're professional WHY. I believe the next step is knowing what kind of professional environment is the best for your God given purpose. However, that's not what most of us do, we research which companies have competitive salaries, have the most benefits, or give the most clout, all superficial benefits that won't fulfill us and bring us joy. Then we complain that we hate our boss, can't stand our co-workers, and admit that our environment is nothing but toxic.

The point is, we have to be more open to putting a more substantial focus on companies who believe what we believe and not just who will give a high paycheck. We must research how they grow, where they invest, employee morale, visions, and missions. These should align with who God says we are and then pray about your next step. The timing of when we enter a new environment that we feel we are being called to is so important because sometimes when God is birthing something out of us, He keeps us in certain toxic situations for a season. However, once that season is up, you have to be willing to get up and grow. We have to be silent enough to know which season we are currently in. I want you to pray about if you are waiting on Him or if He is waiting for you.

I sat on a job for three years after I decided it was time to go. I spent many days begging God to open the door for me to leave. He was teaching me patience, He was building my relationship with my mentor, and he was stretching my imagination and giving me the freedom to explore other avenues with a sure paycheck and a light caseload. The first production I ever wrote, I did it while I was on that job I hated because I had the freedom of summers off and the flexibility of getting off at 3 to pull it off. So sincerely ask God what it is he needs you to accomplish and learn in this season while preparing you for the next.

My next 9-5 that gave me all the feel-goods that I talked about earlier, they had a company culture like none other. I saw young people leading and I saw opportunities for growth. I witnessed innovation and customer service at its best, and employee morale was at an all-time high. No one ran out to leave at five o'clock. If you left at six o'clock, people asked if you were calling it an early night! Working there was a new kind of routine, and I liked it!

So please know that the answer to a toxic nine-to-five isn't always entrepreneurship, and it also doesn't always result in leaving right away either. So don't you dare put this book down and quit tomorrow. What I would like you to do if you don't feel you are where God wants you to be. Write down your why and what you believe and then start to find your people. Research, Google, or ask a friend, no matter where they are in the world, I assure you, your tribe is out there.

ENTREPRENEURS

How to Find Your tribe

One of the main reasons we struggle to get our companies off the ground is we don't know our audience. Every time someone asks who our product or service is for- we say that everybody can use it. The truth is there are a lot of people who don't want what we sell. That's just the facts. My sister paid close to three times the price to go on a cruise because she said the other one didn't provide the same caliber of service as the one she chose. You hear me, three times the price, for companies selling the same product! Therefore the first step is to acknowledge You have a target market.

So who are your people?

Think back to that first time you served someone who was SUPER grateful for your product or service. These customers sang your praises, referred a friend, took the time to shout you out on social media, and used your services again and again. That's your target market. It's essential to specifically know who you are talking to, so that every time you seek to communicate with your audience, you target the areas they frequent. Knowing your audience also helps you to use the kind of language that they can relate to and showcase the aesthetics that they love. One of Apple's key target markets is teenagers. Although Apple is a premium brand, its common knowledge that younger generations feed off technology and, therefore the wealthier and younger demographic will tend to be drawn to this brand. Having a target market doesn't mean that people who don't fall in this category won't buy from Apple; it merely means that this will be a large percentage of their consumers, so they should constantly ensure that they are communicating with them.

When understanding your target market, it is important to know our cousins, best friends, and co-workers may be the last ones to jump on the train. Stop wasting your time venting about their non-supporting butts in your friend chat groups and go out there and serve your people. People are waiting and willing to champion what you bring to the table. However, if you can't identify at least one person who has ever supported what you do, then maybe you don' t have a business.

However, if you have a few good people who have supported what you do, continue to serve them well. I want you to make sure they become a client for life. It doesn't mean many annoying emails asking when they want to use your services again; it involves finding out what they need. What's hard for them right now? What's lacking? What are their concerns when it comes to the areas that you deliver? If you do skincare, consistently have conversations with your people about their interests. What's working, what's not, what are they currently doing? Sooner or later, they will want you to educate them. Give them the facts and provide yourself as an option to solve their problems. Why an option and not the only solution, because you want to be transparent that you understand they have choices, and you want the best for them as a whole, not just what's best for you. This rapport will help people to trust you, and people who trust you become loyal clients and loyal clients affect your bottom line.

How can you find more ?

So you've got a few clients, and that's all well and good, but a few clients won't pay the bills. So I'm going to give you some advice I give to myself. Stop trying to be a celebrity and serve the people who needs you were created to meet! Social media has gotten us caught up in likes and followers, when none of those are the purpose or why God told you to start a business in the first place.

Follow the people who fuel what you believe and give value, so the people who need what you bring begin to see you, regardless of what your follower count is, success will follow you. People are SMART! They smell a fake; they know if you value their support or if you are seeking fame and status. It happens to a lot of us, so if this word is convicting you, don't be ashamed. God keeps reminding me that He is the light, and He won't bring more people if I only see them as fans and not souls. God has blessed some of you women to change the whole world with your hands, don't take that for granted.

Team Builders And Entrepreneurs
How to love your tribe hard:
Be consistent

Ever heard the phrase- out of sight out of mind? You have to keep championing your product/service, no matter how many times you do it because most people in the world are waiting to follow when it is safe. There are a small fraction of people who get on board the first time. No one is an overnight success. Beyonce didn't just pop up one day as the icon she is now. She was on *Star Search* a the age of twelve. That's right twelve. What were you doing at twelve? Star search was a big deal back then too, so who knows how old she was when she started singing in local talent shows. The crazy thing is, she lost *Star Search*. But when we have a slow month of sales, we are ready to quit. What if Beyonce stopped at fifteen? She didn't record her first solo album until she was twenty-one. Almost ten years after her *Star Search* loss. She was consistent!

Bring Growing Value

Game recognizes game. I promise you if you strive to be the best, invest in your craft, it will change the game. We must listen to our audience and continue to grow our products or services to a level that the leaders in our industry are giving, then people can't help but recognize you. I was watching a seminar once where the speaker said,

"Stop playing and Go Pro!" Man, that cut me, but it was true! You aren't growing your business like a professional. I had to have a real talk with myself. I said Kerel, "Your branding is subpar". Your marketing materials are all in your head. You refuse to pay for a website, social media manager, an assistant, a professional work area, professional labeling, but yet still wondering why more people won't come up off their coins? No! It's because you refuse to grow. The old wise saying is right, you have to spend money to make money, and too many of us don't want to do what it takes to invest back into the business.

Innovate and Collaborate

There is a slang we use in the Bahamas when someone is doing something awesome, we say, "I see you!!!" The reason it's been so hard for us to grow our clientele is that we aren't delivering a product or service that's easy for people to see. We've got potential! Like that boyfriend, you are trying to turn into a husband, full of POTENTIAL, but he isn't quite the right fit. That's how the people who want to rock with us feel like we're almost there, but we need to have just a little more professionalism before they really can believe and become a champion for what we do.

We need to do a little more before "they see us." But before they see us, the person who has always seen us and is more ready for us to step up to the plate is our Father in heaven who called us into this meaningful work in the first place. The question is; Is He pleased with the steps we are too afraid to take? Is He sad that we don't have the faith to trust how a hired assistant will get paid when He told us to bring one on a year ago? Or that we won't apply for that particular job because it seems out of our league. I want you to be clear on what I'm trying to say. It's not about trying to impress potential clients or gain fancy jobs. You are working for an audience of one. However, sometimes the people He has attached to our gifts can't recognize us because we currently look nothing like the person He challenged us to be or the person He told them to invest in or hire. Grow and bring value, and I guarantee you your people WILL find you!

117

Colossians 3:23 NIV- *"Whatever you do, do your work heartily, as for the Lord rather than for men."*

My mom spent the first part of her career as an educator in the school system, she then spent years running her Bridal store. Her final role before retirement came when she was recruited to become a full-time Educational Officer. So as you can see, our life's work may look different at various seasons throughout our life. Ultimately, your professional path has to be a discussion between you and God. Let Him lead you toward the meaningful work He has designed for you.

So those of you feeling stuck at work, I pray you to stop dreading Mondays, start taking leaps, and, most importantly, keeping God at the center of everything you decide to pursue!

🔦 CRACK THE CODE:

1. Describe the kind of team you want to work on or describe the type of person you were created to serve? Be specific; Age, sex, location, salary, interest, values, books they read, podcasts they like, conferences they attend. Who are they?

2. Are you an entrepreneur, team builder, or both? How do you know?

3. What is one thing you can do differently to go pro on your "9 to 5" or as an entrepreneur?

👑 QUEEN HACKS:

> Entrepreneurs Read - *E- Myth: Why most small businesses don't work and what to do about it - - by Michael E Gerber*

> Team Builders Read - *Start with Why- by Simon Sinek*

> Entrepreneurs Tip - When you hire - start with freelance employees, then a full-time employee who can do what you can't do. Then make sure they can make you up to two times more money than what they make in a salary, then it's time to expand.

> Team Builders Tip - Research growth conferences, sometimes, your employer is willing to pay part of or all of the expenses because they have a training budget, and just no time to organize the attendance.

CHAPTER 12

SUCCESS LEAVES CLUES FOR YOU

The people who crazy enough to think that they
can change the world, are usually the ones who do

- Steve Jobs

Before we talk about what are the clues and where you can find them. I want us to define what success looks like when God is the foundation. Success for a daughter of the King solely resides in the pursuit and completion of your God-given assignment, becoming the highest version of yourself! As Myles Munroe said, "die empty," do everything God created you to do before you die. It's not tied to a certain amount of Instagram followers, a certain level of monetary wealth, or fame, even though these are the ways we are often tempted to define it. As we pointed out in the first half of this book, if it ain't a purpose, it's pointless.

Hear me right, I don't think God wants us to be purposeful and broke! We have seen many times God has promoted and placed His people at a high level of power, influence, and wealth. King David went from the field to the throne. Moses went from a murderer to a great leader. Joseph went from the pit and prison to the palace, and

120

Esther went from being an orphan to becoming a Queen. Make no mistake, what's for you will be for you! However, our focus can't be on the final destination, because that is the quickest way for us NOT to arrive there. Our focus must be on Him! His methods may seem unconventional, sacrificial, or overwhelming at times, but trust me, the promise is still there!

I want you to know that God can dream a bigger dream for you than you can imagine for yourself. So how do successful people do it?

They follow the clues. Success always leaves clues for you!

Never stop Learning

Successful people are always learning something new. Social Media has catapulted us into such a "fame" culture. The minute we receive a certain level of following, we deem ourselves an expert and become too afraid to admit when we don't know the answers. Seriously STOP pretending you know all the answers. You don't, and that's ok! None of us do! We are often amazed by the amount of wisdom and insight that Oprah has, but don't you realize while being a phenomena/ Talk show host and icon, she has also been a student the entire time. Oprah knew her strength laid in asking people the kind of questions that made them dig more in-depth, allowing them to think on a more significant introspective level. The more questions she asked, the more insight she received and in turn, continued to learn. She was paid to ask questions and absorb wisdom from some of the most influential people around the world. She retained this knowledge and built on it because she knew the key to growing and winning was to commit to continual learning. Think about the wealth of knowledge she gained from all the books she has read, Oprah was humble enough to know that one of the keys to success was in the commitment to be ever-growing and ever learning.

The average CEO reads five books a month, for the last few years I have been trying to master at least one book a month! So why isn't learning a priority for us? We live in the tech world, a world that is always changing.

I sat in a tech conference once and heard the speaker say by the time he wakes up the next morning, something in the tech world has already changed. That's how fast it happens. Therefore you can't know everything. So be open to admitting when you don't know and commit to continual learning, so that you can continue to grow!

Below I have included a list that helps me to grow! Check it out and evaluate how one or all of these tools could help you in your daily life.

Books – New goal two books a month

Podcast - 3-4 episodes a week

Youtube - At least once a day

Conferences - 2-3 a year

Online Courses - Varies(depending on cost and length of the course)

Mentorship/ Coach - At least once a month check-in

Discipline

Let's face it whether we want to admit it or not, successful people are disciplined. Some of you read the list and said, ok cool, I'm doing some of those already, maybe I need to look into one or two or more. Others may have looked and wondered when they would find time to do those things.

We want the results, but we don't want to do the work. When I say "we" I am including myself in this, as I had to place Instagram down for the fourth time to get back to this chapter. We allow social media, Netflix and chill, and idle time with friends to take up ALL of our free time. I'm not saying there isn't a time and place for these moments in our lives; I'm asking you to think about how you are structuring your day.

So whether you have a full-time job or you work for yourself, I want you to think about how many free hours you have in the day outside of work and sleep?

For me, it's roughly 8 -9 hours outside of scheduled work time.

122

Write Down 3-5 Short or Long-term Goals: (For Me) -
Publish May I call You Queen - Short-term
Move into new office space and hire an assistant - short-term
Invited to a big women's conference as a speaker - Long-term
New York Times Bestseller - Long-term
Get Married & Start a family - Long-term

Then I want you to think about your values while thinking of this list because your values should also align with short term and long term goals. Even though I value friendship, it's not a top-five priority for me now, as I am in the early stages of entrepreneurship, so one of the things I do, is try to surround myself with friends who also value the things on my list. Therefore I remain disciplined in my pursuit of success.

Values For Me:
Faith
Family
Purpose - Meaningful Work
Growth
Health

The next thing I want you to do is to try to tie at least something you do throughout the day toward the things you say that you value.

Devotion - Faith
Dinner/ Connect with Parents - Family
Island Dreams Management - Purpose
Listen to Podcast, Read, Youtube, Online Course - Growth
Gym/ Eating Schedule- Health

So how do I fit all of this into one day:

Typical Schedule
5am - 6am - Morning Devotion/ Prep for the Gym
6am - 7am - Gym Time
7am - 8am - Healthy Breakfast connect with Parents
8am - 9am - Get ready for work - Listen to Podcast or Youtube
9am - 5pm - Island Dreams Work/ Special Projects
5:30pm - 6:30 pm - Dinner connect with family

6:30 pm - 7:30 pm - Community Organizations/ Reading Time
7:30pm - 8:30 pm - Special projects i.e. work on book or listen to read
8:30pm - 9:00pm - Get ready for bed, unwind skincare routine

On the best days, my weekdays look like this. On the worst days it doesn't. But, what I found is that this happens the most when I start my week off right. Making the most out of my Sundays is a critical factor in accomplishing weekly goals. Filing my calendar out at the beginning of the week, Meal Prep completed, the Hair regimen, Full Skin regimen all done to make the transition into the work week a little easier.

Saturdays are the days I schedule time to relax, take a break, and bring some balance into my life by indulging in a few things I enjoy. So what does your week look like, or better yet, how do you want it to look?

Discipline means sacrificing going with the flow every day for structure and productivity. It's investing that money into your goals and dreams, instead of being clicker happy- filling your closet with clothes and shoes with online shopping. No matter how many promises or prophecies you receive, no one is coming to hand you success on a silver platter, if you were never ready to do the work.

So maybe you're sitting here saying, I've made a list and I've tried to schedule them as much as I could, but it still doesn't seem to work. Well, you may be like a lot of other well-intentioned women and me too! You are too EASILY distracted!!

I can go to search for one thing on Instagram or Facebook and end up on one of those things for hours, just scrolling, being nothing but a consumer and not a producer. It's the jokes shared in those Whatsapp groups, the article that leads to that next article that you have to read. Youtube videos of hair and makeup tutorials that are great for the weekend flow, but end up knocking you out your weekday schedule. It's binging on your favorite TV shows or random phone calls that you spend hours on, endless lunch dates or dreaded meetings, all of these things are time zappers.

CEO Mark Cuban said he doesn't take a meeting unless someone is writing a check. We're stuck in meetings that can be just phone calls, and productivity is slipping away. One of the reasons I believe we can't get control and discipline in our lives is that we are reactive and not proactive. Instead of planning and remaining in control of our day, we tend to react to what's in front of us, and consistently watch time slip away.

We want to be better, do better, so why don't we? We refuse to track our progress. If we learn to consistently set short term weekly goals, write them down, and measure if we accomplished them or not, we will be able to gauge if we were successful in achieving that goal. We've heard the saying; "If it's not written, it won't get done!" We have to be realistic about where we are now and where we feel led to go and understand the commitment it takes to get there. Get a coach or accountability partner in the areas where it's hard for you to remain focused and attack it with everything in you! Sometimes God is just sitting there waiting, saying to you, YOUR MOVE!

Authenticity

Successful people are authentic. We live in the information generation. There has never been a time where people had this much access to our personal lives. It takes two seconds for someone to forward a private photo, screenshot a conversation, or save a voice recording. The saying "whatever is done in the dark will come to light" has never been more accurate. When sharing their stories, to take power back people have led with their mistakes, failures, and shortcomings. It's no longer something to be ashamed of but something some people are open enough to say that they have overcome.

In my first book, being from a small island, people were shocked that I revealed that I was no longer a virgin. However the people filled with shock weren't my concern, I wrote it for every other girl who wanted to wait, broke the promise she made to herself and wondered how she could ever continue to evolve into the woman she was destined to become. You're not counted out because you made some detours along the way, you are more relatable than you think.

Sarah Jakes Roberts can reach teen mothers more effectively than I ever could. Jackie Hill Perry can relate to women struggling with their sexuality better than most, while Gabrielle Union can connect to hopeful mothers battling infertility on a different level than those of us who have never experienced the pain. There is a way that the painful moments of your life, the ones you're ashamed of, or may make you act different, talk different or walk different can hit someone's heart, they're just waiting for you to share your story. This story lets them know that they're not alone; there is someone who knows what they're going through, and your strength is what will give them the power to carry on. Hear what I'm saying -sharing your story doesn't make you famous, it makes you purposeful. Try writing down the most authentic version of yourself, use my version below as a key.

I am a child of God who hasn't always walked the straight and narrow. I've had my heartbroken and broken some hearts along the way. I've betrayed friends, but also came through for them in some of their darkest hours. I'm loud, I'll hit you when I laugh, some people are overwhelmed by my energy, and I come alive when I hit the stage. I'm a storyteller, and writing eases my soul. My goal in life is to inspire others to become the most authentic version of themselves and value growth while doing it. I'm a 34-year-old Bahamian woman, single, no children, and still live at home with my mama (this statement has often been hard to admit.) I'm building a brand as an entrepreneur as I watch and wait on God to produce an abundance of fruit from my labor; through it all, I know God is faithful!! This statement is the most authentic version of me!

Risk Takers

How do you know if the destination is sent by God versus a motive for success defined by you? When it's a God thing, no matter how painful it is, you will be willing to sacrifice it. Most of you may be thinking, let it go, no that's showing lack of faith, lack of hope in the promise, why would I sacrifice the very thing I truly believe God promised me. Being willing to sacrifice it shows God that while I want to dwell in your promises, I want you more than I want success.

Think about it, Esther in the Bible, she spent all that time going through beauty treatments to get to her destination as Queen. She gets there, and then her uncle tells her to meet with the King and tell him what his most trusted advisor has done so that she can save her people. Esther is super confused, she finally got the thing she worked so hard for, now her uncle wants her to approach the King uninvited which usually leads to death, to give a negative report about his most trusted servant? Like how, that doesn't even make sense! Her uncle then tells her, who knows, maybe you have been called for such a time as this. In other words, as a Jew, you are the only one who understands our plight and have made it to this level in the Kingdom. There is no one else with this unique story. If you die, you die, but making an effort to save your people is a part of what you are in this position to do. So she did, and she didn't die. It became a great defining moment for her in history.

I think what gets us confused about success is that we believe it's about us. We believe God wants to give us all of these fantastic things simply because we are His children and He wants to see us happy. No boo, it doesn't work that way in the Kingdom. While God cares about our well being, his purpose lies in using our lives to tell others about His goodness.

Being a Jew didn't close Esther's rights to the throne. Instead, it's the thing that made her legacy stronger. She thought her Uncle was trying to take something away from her. How can a loving God allow her to get this far, for it only to lead to death? This request didn't make any sense, but in the end: PLOT TWIST! It did make sense, but she risked it all for purpose anyway! So what risk are you afraid to take that can potentially be setting you up to win.

Embrace Failure

We've heard a million stories of successful people getting turned down by 40 banks, sleeping in their cars, living on couches, being told they are too ugly, too old, not the right color, and yet they kept going. Yvonne Orji from the TV show, *Insecure* had a Master's degree in Health Insurance and told her Nigerian parents she was moving to New York to be a comedian. They thought she was crazy. Worse, she spent the next 6-7 years awaiting her "BIG BREAK!" You know how long 6-7 years is being broke, doing countless Youtube videos with minimal viewership but remaining consistent! If this isn't embracing failure, I don't know what it is. The crazy thing is, it was one of those youtube videos that she did years before she got her break out audition that reminded the showrunner Issa Rae about her.

That's the thing about successful people; they know that the struggles while they wait are all a part of the process. They understand that every "overnight success" is ten years in the making — ten years of going at it, working for it. Not just settling for what's comfortable because you have made up your mind things will never get better.

You fight through the fear that it won't happen for you, and maybe you won't get it this time. It doesn't mean it won't happen another way; it doesn't mean there isn't a door waiting to be opened up for you.

When was the last time you tried something new? Last year I learned how to play chess, and I can't believe how much I love the game and business opportunities that came out of it. I was trying to try something new, and out of nowhere, it led to other opportunities. It wasn't easy starting, and no one was out there teaching adults, so I went to a high school after-school program and got my butt kicked in chess from a bunch of teenagers every day. I didn't care. I was learning a new skill, no matter how many times I lost, I was building my stamina! You never know how that new thing you are afraid to try will lead you closer to God's purpose for you. Yvonne Orji discovered her love for comedy when she entered a beauty pageant to win some scholarship money! The very thing that God is waiting to birth in you can be in a new opportunity. Don't be afraid to embrace failing at all costs.

Always learning, discipline, authenticity, risk-taking and embracing failure aren't the only clues left by successful people. Still, they are the few that I have noticed and want to encourage you to try. I also want to help you not to despise this season of trying because, as we said, it's not about the destination, it's about the journey along the way. One of my favorite scripture verses comes from **Ecclesiastes 3:11 NIV**. *"He has made everything beautiful in its time. He has also set eternity in the human heart, yet no one can fathom what God has done from beginning to end."*

I always thought this meant, hang on, don't lose hope, everything you have been waiting for will soon happen, and in that time, life will finally be beautiful. Recently the Holy Spirit had me look at the scripture again and the Spirit made me realize that you are not waiting for everything to be fair. He wants me to see that everything is already beautiful. The moments of disappointments, the struggles, the pains are uncomfortable at the moment, but they are a part of the gorgeous thread in your story.

I may not be living in the condo or home of my dreams yet, but you know what is beautiful - getting to spend these precious moments with my mother and father everyday.

I may not be internationally known as a New York Times bestseller or a motivational speaker yet. Still, you know what's beautiful - having the time to serve my local community one-on-one.

I may not have the husband and family I prayed for, yet. Still, you know what's beautiful -having the energy and time to pump so many hours into building my brand and fulfilling my God-ordained purpose without any other obligations.

Queen, your life is beautiful and as long as you keep Christ first, His version of success for you, will not escape you!

♥ CRACK THE CODE:

1. Write down your own three personal "I may not have achieved this yet" statements, followed by something you currently get the chance to do, which makes your life equally as beautiful.

2. If you didn't take the time to fill out your Goals/ Values/ Activity & daily schedule list, be sure to do it now and try to stay as disciplined as possible

♛ QUEEN HACKS:

> If certain apps like Facebook, Instagram, Whatsapp, or Pinterest are getting in the way of your productivity, remove the icon six screens away from the home screen, so you have to swipe several times to get there. Also, set a screen timer for each app. Therefore, the app shuts down every time you have reached your personal time limit.

> Can't seem to find the time to listen to podcasts, YouTube series or read (audiobooks)? Learn to multitask, listen while you are driving, cleaning, meal prepping, or doing a skin or hair regimen. Kill two birds with one stone!

EPILOGUE

So in case you haven't realized, Christ is the one who's been asking to call you Queen. The great thing about Him granting you this title is that it's a title you don't have to earn, but one He freely gives once you are willing to accept Him as Lord over your life. The joy that comes with wearing His crown is forever. The feeling isn't fleeting or temporary. The love He has for you, the world didn't give it, and the world could never take it away.

So when you get discouraged, overwhelmed, and confused about this journey called life, flip to the back of this book for the **CHEAT CODE**. As humans, the things that we are tempted to idolize will find their way near our hearts, but we must remember:

SURRENDER - Stop asking God to bless our plans and remember to sit, read his word, and pray about how to live out the amazing plans /He has designed for us. Wake up every day, asking Him what He wants you to do. Asking God to bless your plans is like going to work and telling your boss what to do. Instead of following the guidelines He has laid out for you, it just doesn't work that way with your boss or with God.

Matthew 6:33 – *Seek ye first the kingdom of God and his righteousness, and all these things shall be added unto you.*

CONTENTMENT - In every state that you find yourself, be content. Living in the past will make you depressed, while focusing on the future will make you anxious. Learn to live in the now; see the beauty in this season. Be grateful for the blessings you currently have, and watch God bless you with more.

Philippians 4:11 – *I am not saying this because I am in need, for I have learned to be content whatever the circumstances.*

DO THE WORK - Every season will have its challenges. However, faith without works is dead. If you don't learn to do the work you are resenting in the current season, you won't be able to do the work in the season you think will bring you joy. Joy doesn't come when we're stagnant; we see joy when we are continually growing.

Genesis 3:19 - *By the sweat of your brow, you will eat your food until you return to the ground, since from it you were taken; for dust you are and to dust you will return.*

So if you skipped the "Crack the Code" questions and "Queen Hacks," go back and get them done. I want to be honest; these words on these pages may motivate you for a season, but doing the work to discover *your* truth, is the thing that will have you making life-changing decisions.

I want you to know that our REAL best life is in heaven with our father, so until we meet Him, our best life on earth involves an experience on fire for Him alone. Trusting God with your life may seem like an overwhelming commitment until we realize that these external factors could never fulfill us the way Christ can.

I've chased many earthly crowns and, the final one I want to share with you, happened in 2008 during the Miss Bahamas World pageant. The announcer called the last name in the Top 5 and the curtain came down hiding the faces of all of us who didn't make the cut. My goal of becoming Miss Bahamas World was over, and I felt defeated. I never got to compete in the Miss World pageant, never got to train in Puerto Rico, or experience the all-expense-paid trip to New York that I spent months idolizing over. And although I went on to compete in various other pageants, seeking to vindicate the pain I had from this loss, God gave me the best title he ever could on that same night.

It was the *Beauty with a Purpose Award*. This journey wasn't about a physical crown; it was about purpose. Discovering my God-ordained purpose opened more doors than I could ever dream of and more than any physical crown ever could. Sis, I don't know what material or metaphorical crowns you've been chasing, but I just wanted to stop by to tell you that there's always been a spiritual one waiting for you.

May I call I you Queen?

BIBLIOGRAPHY SECTION

Bacon, N. (2018, June 4th). How to Improve Your Mindset. Retrieved from https://nataliebacon.com/how-to-improve-your-mindset/

Carmicheal, E. (2018, November 19th). "You Can Work Harder Than That!|"| Kobe Bryant (@kobebryant). Retrieved from https://www.youtube.com/watch?v=6PDCnhNc2QI&t=527s

Daniels, D. (2018, August 7th). Where is Bae. Retrieved from https://www.youtube.com/watch?v=VsWMQ4XKOOc&t=8s

Inside Edition. (2017, November 30th). See Meghan Markle on '90s Nickelodeon Show After Protesting Commercial. Retrieved from https://www.youtube.com/watch?v=tfaGleA4qYo

OWN. (2018, December 6th). What Dwayne Wade Told Wife Gabrielle Union After Multiple Miscarriages SuperSoul Sunday| OWN. Retrieved from https://www.youtube.com/watch?v=Y7S9rBLD_1I

Ready4eternity. (2017, July 1st). Why Francis Chan Left His Mega Church. Retrieved from https://www.youtube.com/watch?v=VyZx_SSOyfI

Sinek, S. (2009). Start with why: How great leaders inspire everyone to take action. New York, N.Y.: Portfolio.

"sweet spot" *Merriam-Webster.com.* 2019. https://www.merriam-webster.com (1 October 2019)

TED. (2010, May 4th). How Great Leaders Inspire Action | Simon
Sinek. Retrieved from
https://www.youtube.com/watch?v=qp0HIF3SfI4

Youth America. Who is Michael Todd | Interview with Grant
Pankratz at Youth America Leadership Conference. Retrieved from
https://www.youtube.com/watch?v=ZRPX6bNu8I8&t=1078s

Your Fertility. Fertility Factors: Timing. Retrieved from:
https://www.yourfertility.org.au/everyone/timing

Made in the USA
Columbia, SC
14 January 2020